INDIA INSISTENT

INDIA INSISTENT

SIR HARCOURT BUTLER

GYAN

Published by

GYAN

Gyan Publishing House
5, Ansari Road
Daryaganj, New Delhi-110002
Phone: 011-47034999, 9811692060
E-mail: books@gyanbooks.com

Distribution Network
gyanbooks.com
India, USA, Canada, UK, Australia

ISBN: 978-93-7014-161-2 (HB)

First Published, 1931

2nd Impression 2025

Printed at: Gyan Press, Delhi.

INDIA INSISTENT
Author: SIR HARCOURT BUTLER

INDIA
INSISTENT

INDIA INSISTENT

BY

SIR HARCOURT BUTLER

G.C.S.I., G.C.I.E., D.C.L.

CONTENTS

PREFACE

IT has been represented to me from many quarters that a short and simple description of India and its problems would be welcomed by many who have not the time to study reports or standard works. In the following pages will be found the results of much study, the reflections and conclusions of thirty-eight years' service in India. Of this period eighteen years were spent in direct and daily contact with the people, seven in the government of India, and nearly thirteen at the head of the government of two provinces, the United Provinces and Burma.

My experience has left upon my mind a deep impression of the conservatism of India and of the need for caution in political advance on western lines. Without advocating reversal of policy at the present time one need not subscribe to the doctrine that the hands of the clock can never be put back. Indeed, the putting back of the hands of the clock would seem to be a perennial process of history; how else can one explain why the world has advanced so little in so long a time? The Government of India Act of 1919 certainly contemplated the possibility of retrogression, and if responsible government be given prematurely to India, the hands of the clock will surely be put back very sharply. After all, to quote the great historian, Stubbs, "such by-words as reaction and progress are but the political slang which each side uses to express their aversions and professions." My own political faith is that India requires a steady progressive policy, but, even more, a firm and efficient administration. For this I give some reasons in my last chapter. Of late, the administration has unquestionably been subordinated to policy and the results have not been good. They found, it may be hoped, their climacteric in the recent horrors and atrocities of Cawnpore. Sir Henry Maine once observed that the difficulty of governing India lay in the problem of keeping one's clocks in time in two distant longitudes. We cannot change suddenly from Greenwich to Indian time.

In the following pages much has been sacrificed to brevity. If this essay should lead any on to the magnificent treasure-house of fact and comment in the Simon commission's report, it will not have been written in vain.

I

THE LAND AND THE PEOPLE

It is hard to convey to those who have not seen and felt them the vastness and variety of India. The journey by express train from Madras, at the south-east, to Peshawar, at the north-west, takes four and a half days, travelling night and day, and crosses half a dozen countries of the size of first-rate European states, the people of which cannot understand each other's speech. North to south, India is two thousand miles long; at its greatest breadth it is rather more. Its climates range from the icy cold of the Himalayan mountains, whose peaks are wrapped in perpetual snow, to tropical moisture-laden heat only eight degrees above the equator. Its population, which numbers three hundred and fifty millions, speaking twelve main languages and over two hundred dialects, resembles a human aviary with its brilliant colours and strange cries. It includes the fierce Pathan of the north-west, the fiery little Gurkha of the north-east, the subtle intellectual Brahman, the bearded Moslem, the chivalrous Rajput with his feudal ways, the once marauding Mahratta, a mass of darker men who till the soil or are engaged in service, and aboriginal tribes, who shun the daylight, are at home in trees and shoot one another with bows and arrows. Some are tall, some are stunted; some have handsome aquiline features, others are square-headed and broad-nosed; some are almost white, the majority are brown, some again are coal-black. To the flat-roofed and walled city of Peshawar, a central Asian city in appearance, shaggy camel caravans bring the carpets, skins and news of Turkestan and beyond. In the Darjeeling bazaar, clinging on the hillside, almost in the shadow of Kanchanjanga (28,146 feet) the lamas of Tibet and the pedlars of China compare notes of their countries and what they have seen on the way. In the busy marts of Calcutta and Bombay are gathered representatives of every race and every clime. Ethnologically, India is a welter of humanity such as can hardly be found elsewhere.

Scientists divide the people into three principal groups. The *Indo-Aryans*, Brahmans and Rajputs and Sikhs of true descent, have height, long faces and noses and light brown skins. The *Dravidians*, in southern and central India, are shorter, have noses like negroes and dark skins almost black. The *Mongoloids*, near Tibet and in Burma, have greatly influenced the population of Bengal and Assam, and resemble the Chinese, with slanting eyes and yellow skins. The inter-breeding of these groups produced various subgroups classified as Aryo-Dravidian, Mongolo-Dravidian and Scytho-Dravidian. The last sub-group is supposed to include the Mahrattas of the Deccan and the Jats of northern India. The Afghans and Beluchis belong to the Turko-Iranian group. The former are still often connected with the lost tribes of Israel whom in appearance they seem to resemble. This grouping is useful enough as a general guide, but it is of little practical value. It does not explain the origin of dominant tribes or castes, nor does it coincide with differences of language or religious beliefs.

Geographically, there are three great divisions —plateau, plain and mountain-range. The southern triangular *plateau*, known as the Deccan, rises with a general slope from west to east to the Vindhya mountains of Central India, one of the oldest ranges in the world, worn down, like our Cheviots, by weather and time. Geologists assert that this plateau was once connected by continuous land with Africa, that it has never been submerged and that it existed before life began. Coastal fringes of rice cultivation are bounded by the ghats, literally bathing steps or landing stairs, a name given to the hills which form the retaining walls and buttresses of the plateau. The southern part of the Deccan is sub-tropical, with lagoons, rivers, large forests and an ample rainfall. Its northern part is trap, dry, broken and rocky, with low sugar-loaf hills and fastnesses standing out of the plain, with many patches of stunted or scrub jungle. The second or middle division is the Indo-Gangetic *plain*—fertile, alluvial soil watered by great snow-fed rivers. This in geological time was, we are told, the bed of a sea. The country slopes from the dry, almost treeless and even desert zones of Rajputana and the Punjab on the west, to the moist rice and jute-bearing flats and deltas of Bengal on the east. This rich Indo-Gangetic plain has been the lure to India for successive invaders. The third great division is formed by the *mountain ranges*, about a hundred miles in depth, which cut off the sub-continent from the rest of Asia. From these issue the great river systems of the Indus on the west, the Brahmaputra on the east, and the Ganges in the centre, the first flowing into the Arabian Sea, the other two into the Bay of Bengal. The lofty Himalayas has proved an impassable barrier on the north, but many invaders have poured into India through the north-west, or trickled through the north-east frontier hills.

The seasons succeed one another with an almost monotonous regularity. From March to June, the temperature rises, dry hot winds prevail, the ground is baked, agricultural operations are mostly at a standstill, the sun justifies its old name of "the smiter," nature, man and beast gasp with heat. Even the crows open their beaks and gape. This great heat attracts the moisture-laden currents of the south-west trade winds in a natural indraught. These break against the Himalayas and other mountain ranges and descend in rain. For a few days before this happens the air is heavy and life is hardly bearable. One scans the heavens for clouds, in the hope of relief. The rains break, or the monsoon begins, about the beginning or middle of June, often with thunder and lightning and torrential showers. The word monsoon is an Arabic word meaning seasons. The rainy season lasts until the end of September. The day temperatures fall heavily, the night temperatures to a less degree. With October begins the cold weather, the two coldest months being December and January. The climate in northern India is then bracing except in the middle of the day, when the sun is fierce. At Peshawar one wants thick furs morning and evening. In central and lower India the temperatures are higher and vary less with the season, and in southern India most of the rainfall occurs in the last months of the calendar year. India depends on the monsoon for her harvests and her annual budget is described as a gamble in rain.

Although Calcutta and Bombay are, in population, the second and third cities in the whole

British empire, there are in India comparatively few big towns. There are, in fact, only thirty-four towns with a population of a hundred thousand and over. Nine-tenths of the people live in three-quarters of a million villages. These, in the old highways of invasion, or in desolate country, are far apart on sites easily defensible. In quiet, fertile tracts like Oudh and Bihar, both of which have been called the garden of India, the villages are close together, and new hamlets are continually springing up. In eastern Bengal the rivers take the place of roads and one moves about in boats and canoes. The dwellings stretch along the high banks of the rivers and there is little concentrated village life, a feature which increases the difficulty of administration. In rice-growing tracts liable to inundation, any high and dry ground is chosen for the village site. The people build their own cottages, of mud or bamboo with thatched roofs, or of sun-dried bricks, or, where stone or ruins are locally available, of stone. The well-to-do peasantry are comfortably housed according to their ideas of comfort, which do not allow for fresh air. Window space, where it exists, is very small. Corrugated iron roofs are popular where the rainfall is heavy. In the north-west the houses are better and flat-roofed. The tendency to encroach on vacant space is deeply engrained in the character of the people all over

India and causes much litigation. Round the village site the fields are cultivated intensively and enriched by village manure; the further one goes from the village, as a rule, the poorer is the cultivation. The fields are usually small and separated by raised but narrow boundaries which serve to keep the water from running to waste. Where population is dense, the boundaries are reduced almost to the thickness of a clod. The peasantry have small farms ranging from two acres or even less to fifteen acres or even more, averaging for the whole of India about five acres. Beneath these there is a large landless class, agricultural labourers, who from time to time break out in agrarian risings in the hope of getting land. Usually the village has its own servants, the blacksmith, the carpenter, the watchman, the washerman, the barber, the skinner of dead cattle and so on, who are sometimes still remunerated in kind by doles of grain from the threshing floor. Over the greater part of India, there are no hedges except to mark a lane or some valuable crop, or to protect the fields from the ravages of wild animals.* Irrigation wells are conspicuous with their bullock runs, or creaking Persian wheels.

Features of the landscape are the trees. These are scarce in the drier western zones; in

* The prickly-pear hedges of Gujerat are an exception.

more fertile tracts they abound and give a park-like appearance. Old seats of Moslem administration are surrounded by acres of groves. The Hindu also loves trees, and if he is childless he plants a grove that his name may remain. An old custom, no longer generally observed, decreed that man might not eat of the fruit of his grove till he had married it to a well and conversely that he might not drink of the water of his well until he had married it to a grove, both ceremonies involving the feeing and feeding of Brahmans. So the ancient Hebrew preacher made him pools of water to water therewith the wood that bringeth forth trees.* Most villages have a patch of jungle where the cattle feed, and a village tank where the cattle wallow and the villagers drink diluted sewage. In the moister tracts vegetation is tropical and tangled, palm trees and plantains, huge bamboos and large-leaved trees, festoons and canopies of creepers. The Indian garden is a garden of fruit trees, pomegranates and oranges, guavas and small plums, but, above all, the delicious mango. There are few flowers in the plains of India except those imported from countries outside. But nature compensates with a wealth of flowering trees and shrubs, most of which blossom in the hot weather and refresh the jaded eye—

* *Ecclesiastes II*, 6.

purple, mauve, white and yellow, pink and blue and predominantly red, the flame of the forest, the coral and the cotton trees and the glorious gold mohur (*poinciana regia*).

> Flowers that with a scarlet gleam
> Cover a hundred leagues, and seem
>   To set the hills on fire.

The rivers play a great part in Indian life. They roll their brown silt-laden waters down to the sea, fertilising where their floods are not too rapid and the lighter grains of clay have time to settle over the heavier grains of sand, but terrible in their rage. Then the water comes down in masses like a wall ten feet high or even more, tearing down trees, dwellings and all living things and swirling them along. Where they rush out from the hills they dig many channels for themselves. A small obstruction may deflect a large river to the distance of a mile and more. The most famous Indian river is the sacred Ganges, Mother Ganga, which filters all pollution and will travel over the world potable and pure. Its length from source is 1500 miles as compared with 4500 of the Mississippi and 4000 of the Amazon and Nile. The larger rivers, once navigable for some distance from the sea, are now drained for irrigation, but there is still a busy river life and transport by boat, and the crocodiles and turtles consume the corpses which are thrown into the river by the poor but pious Hindu, who cannot afford the wood for the funeral pyre.

The head-works of a great canal are an impressive sight. A high and powerful dam is run across the river and when water is required, it is let through sluices into the main canal. From this it flows through gates or syphons into the distributaries, which are dug at angles from it, and which range from small canals to ditches, and carry the water to the fields. The tail of a canal, where the irrigable area ends, may be two or three hundred miles from the head-works. Where the levels are easy the water flows straight into the fields; in difficult country it has to be lifted or pumped up on to them. Lining the canals with concrete is expensive but saves about a third of the water which otherwise is lost by percolation. Where there are no rivers, a valley is embanked and a large lake formed by storage of rain-water. Altogether, the government has brought some thirty million acres under irrigation—the area is steadily growing—thus adding enormously to the wealth of the country and protecting it against famine. Rivers and lakes serve another useful purpose in filtered water supplies for the towns. The provision of pure water put an end to cholera but increased the fever death-rate owing to the ineradicable habit of the people to leave the taps running, thereby providing breeding grounds for the malarial mosquito. Water supply had, therefore, to be supplemented by extensive drainage, a costly matter.

The people, like other agricultural folk, lead simple lives. They are poor, but certainly better off than they were forty years ago. Very early they rise to perform their toilet in a field, or ravine, or on the edge of the village tank, their water supply. All day long they work in the fields with occasional rests and pulls at the hookah. At noon when "the sun is silent" there is a siesta in the shade. In the village the women clean the cooking pots, grind the corn, cook the food and gossip to one another, whisking away innumerable flies in an atmosphere made acrid by the smoke of cowdung fuel cakes. The children go to school with their slates and text-books or tend the lean cattle which, in the dry season, seem literally to lick the dust. The low castes live apart and skin the dead animals or look after the scavenging swine. Pariah dogs, "whose home is Asia and whose food is rubbish," abound, and move about furtively or yelp piercingly when things are hurled at them, but serve a useful purpose as scavengers and watch-dogs. The real scavengers outside the towns are kites and vultures, who, in less than fifteen minutes will pick the skinned carcase of an animal clean to the bone. In the evening at "cowdust time" the cattle are driven home by winding lanes. Where the village is not split up into factions, the better classes collect round the headman's house or the village tree and discuss the local news, a case in the courts, it may be, prices, the doings of their neighbours or the local officials, and nowadays quite often a vernacular newspaper is read aloud. When night falls—and twilight is very brief—they go to rest on rough wooden beds with a string mattress. To be seen abroad after dark is to court suspicion of illicit love or crime. The happiest scenes are on the threshing floor when a good harvest has been gathered in heaps and the oxen, muzzled or unmuzzled, move round patiently, treading out the corn.

Scriptural images and phrases come back to mind with a new and vivid appeal—the shadow of a great rock in a weary land: the dry and thirsty land where no water is: the women at the well, or grinding at the mill: the crackling of thorns under a pot: the potter and his wheel: the sower and his seed: the lost sheep and the good shepherd: the little child leading large beasts: the lodge in a garden of cucumbers: the grass and reeds and rushes: the water of life, the willows by the water-courses, the tree beside the waters to which the Psalmist likens the righteous man. In the east, water brings bounty and blessing. Ancient Egyptian, Semitic and Sanskrit writings are full of it, and in the Koran-sharif, the righteous are rewarded in gardens through or under which waters flow. At the end of the hot season when the land is as iron and the sky as brass, and the monsoon bursts in torrents and in a few hours the parched ground becomes a pool and the thirsty land springs of water and everything is once more green, the desert does verily rejoice and blossom as the rose.

Indian sacred books and Indian poetry proclaim the glories of nature, its fearfulness and its fertility. The smiting sun, the floods of the great rivers, the tempests, the desolating famines, the ravages of untameable pestilence have powerfully affected Indian thought and its attitude towards the mysteries of life and death. The brightest passages refer to the fruitfulness of nature, the sunshine and the shower, the seed and the harvest, the loveliness and simplicity of living. Ripeness is all. Very beautiful indeed are the golden cornfields in the blue haze of a cold weather morning in northern India, and the waving, smiling, whispering rice fields of the late autumn. The poem *Bande Mataram (Hail Mother)*, inspired by the green rice fields of Bengal, almost attained the position of a national hymn of revolt against things western. I know nothing more impressive and even terrifying than the vast silences of the Indian forest or the Indian mountain-side when one seems to feel a hand upon the shoulder pulling one back from the unknown. And perhaps in all the world there is nothing quite like the softness of an eastern moon, or the stillness of an eastern night, broken only by the melancholy cry of the prowling jackal* or the throbbing of distant tom-toms that celebrate some village wedding or festival.

The monotony of village life, relieved only by occasional market days, has for centuries been brightened by pilgrimage to sacred places. Here the sins of the pious Hindu are washed away by bathing under priestly guidance in the sacred pool. Hither come traders from all parts to sell their wares, elephants, cattle, horses, fine Dacca muslins and machine-made cotton goods, books, household utensils, toys and all the little articles in daily use among the people. Hither come the maharaja in his glory of elephants and retinue, processions of holy men, naked fakirs, marvels and freaks, calves with five legs, children with two heads, giants, puppet shows and all the appurtenances of the mediæval fair in Europe.

* Every evening at dusk, from Calcutta to Peshawar, the jackals come out from their hiding places of the day and utter their peculiar and piercing cry. It is one of the few signs of unity in India!

Formerly, the pilgrims came in hundreds, on foot or riding, by ox-cart, elephant or boat: now they come in thousands by rail and motor-car. Recently, there were three millions at the religious fair at Allahabad. For months beforehand, great preparations are made for the comfort of these crowds, their lodging, food, water-supply and sanitation. Happy orderly crowds they are in their clashing harmonies of colour, grateful for kindness and attention, enjoying the fun of the fair no less than the religious merit of the outing. But let some religious dissension arise and all is changed in a moment to blows and shouting, vile insults and a tiger-like ferocity that will hurl people alive into flames and dance with joy at the victims' agony.

The census shows less than a tenth of the population as literate, and the ignorance of India is dense to a degree unknown in Europe. Illiteracy is not always or necessarily ignorance. The higher castes have a fund of practical knowledge although they may not be able to write or read. The bard or priest goes round the villages reciting the stories of the great Hindu epics; the maulvi in the month of mourning draws tears and sympathy by reciting the ever-moving tale of the death of Husain. About the year 300 B.C. Megasthenes, a Greek envoy to an Indian court, was impressed with the truthfulness of the Indian people; and it is common experience that in their own villages and before their own people, and if they are not frightened, villagers are generally truthful. In the law courts tutored perjury is all too common; and the annals of village crime are sordid and brutal; but the mass of the people are honest in their own ways and hard-working. In the industrial centres there are blocks of casual or seasonal labour which are undisciplined and disorganised, an easy prey for the agitator. Ignorant people, in all countries, are credulous in an extraordinary degree, and India is no exception to the rule. The wildest rumours gain ready circulation and most malignant and fantastic intentions are attributed to a benevolent authority!

In the towns and, to a less degree, in the countryside, there has grown up an educated class known as the intelligentzia, dissatisfied with its surroundings, critical of foreign influence, and in a hurry for reform, swayed by words and disinclined to connect them with facts or things. This class is no doubt important, but it has been given a quite undue prominence because it can speak and write English fluently and has borrowed the language but not as yet the spirit of English politics. It is the only class that English politicians can understand, or English and foreign visitors to India can converse with. It is a matter of common remark that it is less in touch with the mass of the people and especially the agricultural classes than the corresponding class in any western country. It forms the majority of the legislative assemblies and controls a fairly large press. But the newspapers written in English have little influence compared with the newspapers written in the vernacular which know how to appeal to the Indian mind and can convey their meaning in words and expressions which escape the perception of the ordinary European. Few papers have a circulation of 5,000 copies. As an instance of press influence the *Zemindar*, an *Urdu* paper of the Punjab representing Moslem feeling, rose in circulation from I think 5,000 to over 25,000 copies in less than a month at a time when the Moslems were deeply moved by what was known as the mosque incident at Cawnpore. Many of my Indian friends belong to the intelligentzia; one of my best friends was the late Mr. Moti Lal Nehru, for many years leader of the congress movement. He broke the law and I ordered his prosecution, but even then there was no malice, for he sent me a message that had I known my law better I could have got him eighteen months instead of six! He was a great gentleman and loyal friend, whom I shall always bear in affectionate remembrance while lamenting his political apostasy. As English education spreads the present rather one-sided character of this class will disappear and it will become more representative.

The landowning class, for all their rather arbitrary notions, are in closer touch with the poor men at their gate. This class has not always received the consideration which it deserves. It has, in the management of its estates, an administrative experience of real value. Though less clever than the intelligentzia and much less vocal, it is better able to grip the realities of ordinary life. It is customary to regard this class as heavily in debt and doomed to extinction. But a rough-and-ready enquiry made about ten years ago throughout the United Provinces, with its population now of forty-eight millions, showed that sixty per cent. of the landowners, each paying land revenue to the state of Rs. 5,000 per annum (nearly £400) or over, were altogether free from debt. No other country probably could show an equally prosperous proprietary. The landowning class are conservative as a body, often well equipped in their own literature and language, generally possessing excellent manners. One cannot meet manners to compare for old-world courtesy with those of the courtly Hindu or Moslem aristocrat. The most important, privileged and loyal landowning body is that of the Taluqdars of Oudh, who have fine buildings and their central association in Lucknow, who support worthy institutions liberally and give splendid entertainments. There are quite twenty taluqdars who pay over £10,000 a year in government revenue: their incomes might be taken to be three times that sum. On the whole, they are good indulgent landlords. The more prosperous the landlord the better it is for the tenantry. The poor landlord cannot afford to be generous and "a poor man that oppresseth the poor is like a sweeping rain which leaveth no food."*

Many centuries of autocracy have left indelible marks on Indian and particularly on Hindu mentality. Indians are quick to recognize power in individuals. They are swayed only by power and religion, said an oriental, used to dealing with his own people. "The Asiatic," says Kinglake in *Eothen*, "seems to be animated by a feeling of respect, almost bordering upon affection, for those who have done him any bold and violent wrong."† They take little account

* *Proverbs* 28, 3.

† I could support this view with many illustrations from my own experience. I will take one. When I was a district officer I found a man in my district who terrorised his own neighbourhood. There were several murders to his charge and no evidence could be produced. With the help of a loyal Indian subordinate we broke him. It took over a year, as we had to get rid of some subordinates who were in his pay. In the end he was imprisoned. Later, he came to see me and asked for an appointment for his son on the ground that we were old friends! His son got the appointment and did well and his father became a respectable member of local society!

of human life. Few can face public criticism or fight a losing battle. Trained to speak ingratiatingly to their autocrats, they are apt to say what will please while working for their own ends. At times they are difficult to understand and their words do not always prepare one for their acts. In mental agility the Indian far outstrips the European. When the European thinks that he is getting round the Indian, the Indian is nearly always getting round him. Not in dialectic did it please God, said an old Christian writer, to save his people. The only strength of the European is in direct dealing on perfectly straightforward lines. Indians are suspicious of the European as they are of one another. They resent the aloofness of the European but make many European friends. Human nature is a fairly constant quality all the world over, and it is quite impossible to strike a balance of good qualities and faults. It has been said that all Asiatics are pitiless and yet the divine story of compassion in our literature has reached us from an Asiatic source and concerns a nameless oriental—the good Samaritan. Throughout Asia society is based on the family. Pitiless, it may be, outside the family, within it an Asiatic is often full of pity, and the kindness of Indians to their children is proverbial. There is no poor law in the east. Each family supports its poor. Conversely the pressure of the family is tremendous, and few Asiatics can resist it sufficiently to dispense patronage wisely. To this it may be added that the Indians are as essentially religious as the Europeans are essentially secular. Religion is still the beginning and the end, the alpha and omega of Indian life.

II

THE RELIGIONS OF INDIA

HINDUISM, the religion professed by larger numbers than those professing any other religion in India, has never been authoritatively defined. It includes a social system based on caste, a ritual conducted by Brahmans and many schools of philosophy. It is at once elastic and rigid, "subtle and gross, spiritual and sensual." It has no church, or creeds, or organised ecclesiastical authority. It preaches pantheism, which identifies everything with God, and welcomes polytheism which disintegrates God into many divers forms. For the present purpose, a Hindu may be described as a person born into a social system based on caste, which acknowledges the supremacy of the Brahman caste, and derives its religious sanctions from the Vedas and other ancient sacred books. It is part of practical Hinduism to venerate the cow and give for the majority a low status to women, which does not, however, prevent them from exercising great influence in family or even in public life.

The Vedas, the sacred books of the migrant Aryans, are about 3500 years old. They have much in common with the tenets of the ancient religions of Persia and of Greece. They disclose gods and goddesses personifying the forces of nature such as sun, wind, fire, water; powerful and true, rewarding and punishing; enjoying sacrifices and drinking the intoxicating juice of the soma plant.* In the earliest Vedas there is no certain reference to caste, or to the doctrine of the transmigration of souls, under the retributory law of karma. These came in later, as did the doctrine of the Hindu Trinity. The three gods of this Trinity are Brahma the creator, Vishnu the preserver, and Siva the destroyer. Vishnu has three popular incarnations, Rama, Krishna and Jagannath. The car of Jagannath has passed into the literature of the nations. Siva is often worshipped through one of his wives, especially the cruel and blood-lusting Kali. Hinduism has absorbed much of the indigenous and primitive beliefs of India, such as snake-worship or phallus-worship and found accommodation for innumerable deities. In the well-known lines of Sir Alfred Lyall:

> "Here in this mystical India, the deities hover and swarm,
> Like the wild bees heard in the tree tops, or the gusts of a gathering storm."

The origin of caste is still obscure. Before the

* Sir Aurel Stein has recently given reasons for thinking that this plant may have been wild rhubarb.

dawn of authentic history, the Aryans, a light-coloured race, of European not of Asiatic origin —so modern scholarship conjectures—entered India from the north-west and spread slowly over the Indo-Gangetic plain, afterwards penetrating the southern plateau. The original home of the Aryans is now located somewhere about Hungary. Their first migrations are thought to have taken place in mass, with families and flocks, caused perhaps by one of those convulsive natural changes that make whole populations move. There was, according to M. Sénart, no vestige of a state. These were followed by military invaders who married the darker women of the country, known as Dravidian, the result possibly of a former migration. At what date caste arose cannot be known. There are four traditional castes in the Sanskrit book Manu, (1) the Brahman or priestly, (2) the Kshattrya or kingly and military, (3) the Vaisya or trading and (4) the Sudra or serving. Whether the facts ever corresponded to this division, how and when the division came about, whether it was of Aryan or local origin, whether the family, sub-caste and caste correspond to the family, the clan and the tribe of the Greeks and Romans are points for learned controversy.* The Sanskrit word

* A most interesting discussion will be found in the learned M. Emile Sénart's "Caste in India," translated by Sir E. Denison Ross, C.I.E. (Methuen & Co.).

"varna" literally means "colour," but whether it should be translated as class or caste is in dispute. What is certain is that there are now over two thousand castes and sub-castes, admission to which is by birth alone, the members of one of which cannot intermarry, eat, drink or smoke with the members of another. Marriage must be endogamous within the caste but exogamous outside the sub-caste. It is alleged that some castes and sub-castes have arisen by occupation, some in other ways. The first three of the traditional castes are "twice born," that is, when adolescent, fit to make offerings to the Gods and enter full religious life, they are invested with the sacred thread, worn over the left shoulder to the right hip. This is a slender string formed of nine strands twisted to the right in threes, of cotton for the Brahman, of hemp for the Kshattrya and of wool for the Vaisya.*

The caste is ruled by a president and committee who watch the interests of its members and punish those who violate its rules, by fine, by ordering pilgrimage, by a dinner to the caste, or in extreme cases by exclusion from the caste. This last penalty is complete ostracism. None of his late caste fellows, not even his wife, can eat or drink or smoke with one who is out of caste as long as he is under ban. The ban can be removed

* *Manu II*, 44.

by payment or atonement perhaps involving the consumption of the five products of the cow—milk, curds, clarified butter, urine and dung. New castes or sub-castes are constantly formed or promoted in the social scale with the help of the Brahmans. Aborigines are swept into the caste system by accepting Brahmanic control and an orthodox pedigree or legend to conceal their real origin. The one permanent and persistent fact is the supremacy of the Brahman. Brahmans must be paid and fed on every occasion of festival or ceremony. Brahmans must be treated with almost servile respect, even to the touching of their feet on casual meeting. Any offence against a Brahman is a mortal sin and to kill a Brahman condemns the culprit to an almost interminable series of disgusting or unpleasant transmigrations. There are many kinds of Brahmans of varying status—"As many kinds of Brahmans as of rice"—is an old saying. Only the lower ones will touch the plough themselves. The position of the Brahman is thus one of unparalleled privilege. The basis of caste is purity of birth and ritual. There are relaxations of caste rules in the matters of travel and social intercourse, but in the essential status of marriage as affecting purity of birth and ritual, caste is said by competent observers to be as strict and exclusive as ever it has been.* There are about some hundred and seventy millions of caste Hindus.

Outside the caste system are about seventy-five millions of persons classed as Hindu, but not accepted as such in religious or social life. These are known as the depressed classes and include aboriginal tribes. From time immemorial they have been treated as unclean by the Brahmans. When a Brahman came along they had to get out of his path and announce the presence of pollution with a cry. The observance of this custom is now rare and local, but the pollution remains in Brahman eyes. Even their shadow throws defilement, and if it rests on food, that food must be thrown away. Many have sought refuge in Christianity and Islam. Some caste

* Mr. Vincent Smith concluded that "talk about the abolition or even the automatic extinction of caste is futile. Caste within India cannot be either abolished or extinguished within a measurable time. The system grew up of itself in remote antiquity because it suited India, and will last for untold centuries because it still suits India on the whole, in spite of its many inconveniences. Reformers must be content to make the best of a system which cannot be destroyed. The absolutely indispensable compromises with modern conditions will arrange themselves from time to time, while the huge mass of the Indian agricultural population will continue to walk in the ancestral ways. The deep waters of Hinduism are not easily stirred. Ripples on the surface leave the depths unmoved." —"The Oxford History of India," by Vincent A. Smith, C.I.E., Indian Civil Service retired, Oxford, at the Clarendon Press.

Hindus have now espoused their cause—partly from feelings of humanity, largely from political calculation. In an extended electorate these people will have power. Under British rule they have made great advance and have gained self-respect and influence. Already in Madras they have gained a majority in the legislature and formed an administration. High caste politicians appear with them on public platforms, but admission to ordinary public schools is still generally barred for their children, and all are excluded from the temples of the orthodox. In this connection, quite recently Hindu leaders issued a special appeal in the Bombay presidency. "The present constitution of Hindu society with untouchability," the appeal says, "has been found to be best for metaphysical and social progress" and it asks "political leaders not to dabble in these questions, which will create differences in the Hindu community." The prejudices of centuries are against the depressed classes, but it may well be that Brahmanism, which has adapted itself so often in the past to changing conditions, will, in the end, absorb them on some terms into its fold.*

The orthodox Hindu, not only the Brahman,

* It is time that the term untouchability should be dropped. The progress made demands it. This should be easy for Europeans, who, in the eyes of caste Hindus, are untouchable! A comment, this, on our social aloofness!

believes implicitly in the permanent value of caste. In his eyes it is the most perfect social system conceived by man. Writing at the beginning of the nineteenth century, the Abbé Dubois, than whom no European ever better understood the Hindus, thought that caste had kept the Hindus from relapsing into barbarism, that its advantages more than outbalanced its resulting evils. Speaking at Calcutta in 1916, the Maharaja Dhiraja of Durbhurga glorified caste with "its immutable division of functions" "laid down for all time by our inspired seers and sages to whom the past and the future and the inner working of the human mind were as an open book," "the best and surest safeguard against the spirit of unrest, against the growing bitterness between the classes and the masses, between capital and labour which is constantly menacing western civilisation." "In India," writes professor Rapson, "human institutions have received the sanction of a religion which has been concerned more with the preservation of social order than with the advancement of mankind."*

The sacred books are full of moral precepts and examples, but the keystone of working Hinduism is the doctrine of karma by which a man must reap as he has sown. There are many

* "The Cambridge History of India," Vol. I, page 54.

schools of philosophy but most Hindus believe in transmigration of the soul, through a succession of existences, until by long purification it is fit for absorption into the universal essence, or one reality, the original cause and ultimate goal of all individual souls. This simple system of rewards and punishments permeates the ideas of the people, high and low, wherever Brahmanism has established itself. The village watchman guiding you across the fields will tell you that the soul of the local money-lender will go into pice, a small copper coin. A prayer at the temple was overheard that if the worshipper must be an animal in the next existence he might be an Englishman's dog. The Christian idea of the atonement is crude in Hindu eyes. All matter is evil. The physical world is illusion (maya), quite unsubstantial, "a shadow projected upon the white radiance of eternity." Only by a long process of asceticism and conquest of matter by curbing desire can the Hindu hope to be fit for absorption into the one reality. How else could one find a compensatory balance for the handicaps and inequalities of the caste system?

The ritual is in the hands of Brahmans and is little known to Europeans. Orthodox Hindus say that much of it, handed down orally, has already been lost. In all respectable Hindu houses the day begins with the lighting of the sacred fire. In many large temples gross abuses are prevalent and the priests are sodden with dark corruption. Perhaps the worst abuses are sexual; there seems to be some connection between strong sunlight and sexual activity. To western and eastern eyes alike, there are many sordid things in popular Hinduism. And yet above the impurities and polytheism, there is even for the ignorant an over-spreading idea of one supreme essence, or reality, or God.

The corruption of the priesthood and the tyranny of the caste system have led at different times to great reforming movements. Of these the first known to us was Buddhism. There have been others of local influence. "We find," said Professor Macdonnell, "a general tendency on the part of religious founders, such as Basava, the founder of the Lingayats in the twelfth century, Kabir the founder of the Kabir-panthis in the fifteenth, of Nanak and of Chaitanya in the sixteenth, to proclaim the social equality of all those who entered their order, so as to relax the bonds of caste. In practice, however, it has turned out that this levelling down of caste distinctions has met with only partial and temporary success."* All over India are monasteries of ascetics and fakirs who have thrown off priestly domination and caste, and travel

* "Comparative Religion," Calcutta, 1925.

over the country, living on alms, carrying news, often curing the sick, sometimes making political mischief. Outside these again are saints who win followers by holiness. Several such I have met and remember. One in particular was carried in a palanquin with a train of followers about half a mile long, Moslems as well as Hindus. He preached the doctrine "love one another," gave advice and settled the disputes of his disciples. I dismounted and walked some way by the side of his palanquin in conversation with him. So long as I live I shall never forget the compelling goodness of his face and speech and his overpowering gentleness.

The effect of caste is that all Hindu society has a religious basis. And religion still forbids the removal of much that is admitted to be impure.* Forty years ago, social reform was the cry of giants like Ranade, Telang and Bhandarkar. Child marriage was to be abolished. Widows were to re-marry. The lower forms of religious practice were to be discarded. But orthodoxy strangled social reform. This was especially the case in Bengal. One, who knew Indians intimately and loved them well, and was in spirit half a Hindu, wrote: "The natives know their minds. They don't want freedom and they won't

* Mr. Gandhi said of Miss Mayo's "Mother India" that it opened sewers, that it was a book that every Indian and no European should read.

have social progress. What they will stake their lives on is the caste system, which was divinely instituted thousands of years ago and can never change. That is the civilisation of the hive and the ant-heap. The Bengalee, at any rate, likes it best." A measure to raise the age of marriage has lately been passed by the Indian legislative assembly, largely under the stimulus of Miss Mayo's book. It appears already to have provoked intense opposition in Brahmanic circles. Its enforcement will be partial only, because births are not accurately registered and so it is difficult to prove age. One cannot put policemen into bedrooms and it is scarcely possible to get evidence of what happens in the zenana. The new act has been anticipated by an unusually large crop of premature child marriages, and the Moslems now find that it interferes not with their customs but with their religious law. Nevertheless, the mere passage of a law is a definite step forward. In time a good law may mature into good custom.

Real reform must come from within and it will come slowly. The forces of reaction are stronger than those of progress. The horrors and sadness of child marriage and child widowhood will probably not soon pass away.* Looking to the

* This is the inference to be drawn from the report and evidence of the Indian age of consent committee.

good side of Hinduism, and many Hindus lead noble lives, one cannot deny to it civilising influence in the past. It sent its missionaries into all corners of India, absorbing what it found, good or bad. Over mountains and across rivers, through forests almost impenetrable it has forced its way. It has produced sages and thinkers equal to those of any country, saints and holy men innumerable, wise administrators and large-hearted philanthropists. One evening at Muttra, at the request of the priests, I lifted up the sacred fire, and when I saw the ecstasy which lit up the faces of some thousands of worshippers, I realised that Hinduism, however little one may understand it, brings support and solace ineffable to many millions of our fellowmen.

"Buddhism," says Professor Macdonnell, "was the first religion to overstep the boundaries of nationality and extend morality to its widest sphere, mankind, by means of missionaries sent to foreign countries. It was thus characteristically ascetic, moderate, altruistic, cosmopolitan." Gautama, the Buddha or "Supremely Enlightened One," was born a prince in northern India in the sixth century before Christ. Impressed at an early age by the suffering of the world and the universality of pain, he abandoned his family and took refuge in meditation and an ascetic life. He found enlightenment under a fig tree at Gaya and preached his first sermon at the deer park of Sarnath near Benares.* He repudiated the authority of the Vedas and the Vedic sacrificial system, denied the existence of a world soul or an individual soul, discarded caste in the monastic orders and discouraged metaphysical speculation. On the other hand, he adopted the Hindu doctrines of transmigration and the law of karma, he preached the goal of release from transmigration in a nirvana†—extinction like a lamp—of unbreakable rest. Self-mortification, he said, was as fatal to true spiritual life as self-indulgence. Avoiding both these extremes, a good man seeking truth should follow the middle path which leads to true vision and knowledge, to peace, to super-human insight into the heart of things to all revealing enlightenment and nirvana. There were four noble truths: (1) all that exists is liable to suffering, (2) the origin of suffering is human passions, (3) the cessation of passions releases from suffering, (4) the eightfold path leads to the cessation of suffering, by right views, right resolve, right speech, right deed, right life, right

* It is characteristic of the tolerance of the British empire that in 1922 I, a Christian, laid the foundation stone of a Buddhist shrine in Sarnath next door to Benares, the holy city of orthodox Hinduism.

† Nirvana has been described "as the dying out in the heart of the fell fire of the three cardinal sins, sensuality, ill will and stupidity."

endeavour, right thought and right meditation. In the beginning Buddhism had no place for prayer and sacrifice, but by degrees there grew up the worship of relics and the adoration of sacred sites. Its strength lay in its moral teaching in which it left Brahmanism far behind, and to some extent anticipated Christianity especially in its emphasis on love and joy. Its commandments were five only in number. They forbade the taking of life, theft, unchastity (adultery in the layman, marriage in the monk), lying and intoxicants. On the whole it raised the status of women but still left it none too high. Buddhism lasted a thousand years in India. Expelled by resurgent and triumphant Brahmanism it became outside India, its home, one of the popular religions of the world.* The Burmans are Buddhists, some thirteen millions, but insist that Buddha was a Burman. Only a few years ago in Rangoon a film of the life of Buddha showing

* According to *Whitaker's Almanac* the figures are:

	Millions
Confucians and Taoists	350
Roman Catholics	331
Hindus	230
Moslems	209
Protestant Churches	206
Buddhists	150
Orthodox Catholics	144
Arianists	135
Shintoists	25
Jews	16
Unclassified	50

him as an Indian had to be withdrawn in order to avoid a breach of the peace. Buddhism in Burma sits lightly on the more ancient worship of the spirits, or Nats. Although their religion is in many respects negative, Buddhists are generally cheerful and happy.

Islam is a very powerful religion in India. There are more Moslems in India than in any other country. Islam is a universal religion in its appeal to all mankind and from the first it has set out to make proselytes by suasion or sword. Semitic in origin Islam means resignation to the will of God but is a faith incorporate with force. Islam is as simple and democratic as Hinduism is aristocratic and complex. It rests on sheer monotheism. The five duties of the pious Moslem are (1) to recite the creed ("There is no god but God and Muhammad is his Prophet"), (2) to say his formal prayers five times daily, (3) to fast "in the month of Ramadhan, (4) to give alms, and (5) to perform the hajj or pilgrimage to Mecca. It has been computed that some twenty-five thousand pilgrims go annually from India to Mecca, as compared with forty thousand from Central Africa and the Sudan, thirty thousand from Arabia, thirty thousand also from Malay, Borneo and the Celebes, and fifteen thousand from Egypt. The Moslems of India number about eighty millions but occupy a position more important than their numerical strength. In eastern Bengal, the Punjab, the north-west Frontier Province and Scinde, they are in a majority. In other provinces they are in a minority. They are more virile than the Hindus, partly because their religion is simple and militant, partly because they marry at a later age, while their widows re-marry, and partly because they enjoy a more generous diet including meat. Moreover they have the experience of some centuries of rule in India behind them and they derive inspiration from the Islamic world outside. Islam has many glorious chapters in history and learned Moslem scholars at Baghdad and Cordova kept burning the torch of knowledge and culture when Europe generally was sunk in darkness. Panislamism is perhaps a feeling rather than a force; so difficult is it for the different Moslem peoples to combine, Turk and Arab, Afghan and Egyptian, Persian and Central Asian; but it is unquestionably a sentiment which, at times, produces powerful reactions in India. Strong currents from outside run through the Indian Moslems in periods of excitement, and on the north-west Frontier, Afghans, Pathans and other warlike tribes are waiting for an opportunity to overrun and pillage the fertile plains and rich cities of India.

In the interests of their religion and culture,

the Moslems long adhered to their classical languages, Arabic and Persian, in preference to English. The Hindus thus got the start of them and a virtual monopoly of appointments requiring a knowledge of English. The path of reform was opened for the Moslems by a very great man, Sir Syed Ahmad Khan, who, in the teeth of violent opposition, founded Aligarh College which has now developed into the Moslem university. In response to Moslem demands, separate electorates were granted to them during the Viceroyalty of Lord Minto, a privilege to which they attach continuing and indeed progressive importance. Fortified by English education the Moslems are to-day in a very different position from that which they held fifty years ago. The doctrine of Islam as to the unity of God and the equality of men before God is well known, and at times seems to make it difficult for Moslems to choose and follow a leader. Their other great doctrine is the wickedness of idolatry in any form. The impressiveness of their prayers and the services in their mosques with their movements, prostrations and genuflexions in perfect unison have frequently been described. The call of the muezzin to prayer from a minaret or turret, the performance by the faithful of the five times of prayer, their faces turned towards Mecca, with the perfect precision and doubtless the health-giving advantages of physical exercises, are among the most arresting sounds and sights of the east.

Indian Moslems have been, on the whole, comparatively little touched by the modern movements in Islam. They disapproved as a body of the overthrow of Sultanate and Caliphate. The puritanical Wahabi movement found many followers in India at one time, but its impression has not survived. The Ahmediyah sect has many votaries; and mystics, ascetics and poets rise to more than local influence. The east is ever ready for religious questionings and secessions and the Moslems have their saints and holy men. Indian Moslems are frequently the descendants of converted Hindus. In times of peace between the two communities and in certain parts of the country Hindus and Moslems join in one another's ceremonies and, to some extent, share one another's customs.* The Moslems are regarded as one big caste by the Hindus and, like ourselves, trespassers in India.

Although the number of the Christians is still small, about six millions, Christianity has, through the reading of the Bible and the education and example of the missionaries, exercised a

* My friend the able and learned Mr. Justice Mahmood told me that he was collecting material for a work on the influence of Hinduism on Islam in India. Unfortunately he died without accomplishing his purpose.

profound influence on the mind of India. A Christian church has existed in India for some 1500 years, if not longer. Its progress has been significant enough to stimulate, in opposition to it, the activity of the Arya Samaj in Upper India, a Hindu sect founded by a powerful reformer Swami Dayanand. He preached a return to the Vedas and the abolition of idols, caste and child marriage. The teachings of the cultured missionaries and laymen of Calcutta, Hare and Duff, Carey, Marshman and others, led to the foundation by Raja Ram Mohun Roy and Keshub Chander Sen of the Brahmo Samaj which, however, remains a small community. In the south of India whole tribes and villages of aboriginals and depressed classes have embraced Christianity. The social isolation of the converted Christian and the difficulty of marrying his children is slowly disappearing, and Christianity offers a high status to women. The feeling that Christianity has hitherto been handicapped by the diverse western forms in which it has been propagated will perhaps be met successfully by the recent establishment after long discussion amongst protestant bodies of a united independent Indian church. This is an event of real importance of which the result cannot be foreseen, but it is a reasonable anticipation that an Asiatic church will appeal to

Asiatics in a manner and to a degree that no western church has hitherto been able successfully to appeal.

The Sikhs number only four millions but are important on account of their energy and military qualities and their concentration in one fairly circumscribed geographical area in and near the Punjab, although their business capacity has carried many as traders and contractors and policemen to transmarine employment in different countries. The founder of the religion, Nanak, the first Guru, was born near Lahore in A.D. 1469 and died near Jullundur in 1539. He was thus a contemporary of Martin Luther who was born in 1483 and died in 1546. Like other Hindu reformers, he led a revolt against the power of the priesthood and the rigidity of the caste system and proclaimed the equality of all who entered the new order. He rejected idolatry and the incarnations of the orthodox Hindu gods, preaching that there was one God and one God only. This simple monotheism was accompanied by a belief in the transmigration of souls and predestination. He was followed by nine Gurus who are reverenced by their followers. Their sacred book the *Granth Sahib* is enshrined in the Golden temple at Amritsar. They developed a military spirit and a fiery enthusiasm which were fanned by the hostility and persecution of the Moghuls. The ninth Guru—Teg Bahadur—was killed by Auranzeeb for refusing to embrace Islam. "The history of the Sikhs," says Sir Alfred Lyall, "illustrates a phenomenon well known in Asia, where an insurrectionary movement is always particularly dangerous if it takes a religious complexion, and where fanaticism may endure and accumulate under a spiritual leader until it explodes in the world of politics with the force of dynamite." Under the military genius of Ranjit Singh, the Lion of the Punjab, the dominion of the Sikhs extended to Peshawar and Kashmir. It was finally overcome by the British in 1849. The Sikhs furnish large numbers of recruits for the Indian army: it has been said that but for their connection with the British army they would have before this been reabsorbed, like many other Hindu sectaries, into orthodox Hinduism. They are a proud martial race, who cannot forget that, less than a century ago, they were rulers of a great kingdom. Between them and the Moslems there is fierce hereditary hatred.

The great Akbar in vain sought reconciliation of these warring creeds in one great eclectic faith. The British government in serene toleration, holding no form of creed and contemplating all, gives equal rights to all to practise their own worship. It interferes only when one religious body is aggressive against another. This policy was laid down in Queen Victoria's proclamation of 1858, the charter of Indian liberties. "Firmly relying ourselves," so ran the royal rescript, "on the truth of Christianity and acknowledging with gratitude the solace of religion, we disclaim alike the right and the desire to impose our convictions on any of our subjects. We declare it to be our royal will and pleasure that none be in anywise favoured, none molested or disquieted, by reason of their religion, faith or observances, but that all shall enjoy the equal and impartial protection of the law; and we do strictly charge and enjoin all those who may be in authority under us that they abstain from all interference with the religious belief or worship of any of our subjects on pain of our highest displeasure." That royal policy laid down in noble language has been carried out in spirit and to the letter, but it cannot be said to have guided many footsteps into the paths of religious peace. Indeed, the clashing of religions has increased of late from causes that appear to be resistent and unresponsive to external and secular control.

III

THE INDIAN STATES

THERE are, at present, two Indias, British India, governed by the Crown through laws of Parliament and the Indian legislature, and the Indian states under the suzerainty of the Crown but still for the most part governed by the absolute will of their Princes. The Indian states occupy about two fifths of the area and contain about one fifth of the population of India, excluding Burma. Altogether the population of the Indian states is some eighty millions. The states are the picturesque, the Indian India. Where the Prince is a Rajput and his people are Hindus, the ideal of Brahmanic Hinduism is realised. In the Brahmanic polity of the sacred books the Kshattrya (Rajput) Raja is as necessary an element as the Brahman priest, his legitimate adviser, and all that is corporate in Hindu feeling converges on him. But religious links are often wanting. In most states the population is mixed as in British India. The two largest states in area are Hyderabad and Kashmir. In Hyderabad, the Ruler, "our faithful ally" His Exalted Highness the Nizam, and his government, are predominantly Moslem, while the great majority of his subjects are Hindu; in Kashmir the Ruler, His Highness the Maharaja, and his government, are predominantly Hindu, while the great majority of his subjects are Moslem. Altogether there are one hundred and eight Princes, who are members of the chamber of Princes in their own right, of whom only twelve are Moslems, the remainder being Hindus. These hundred and eight states contain more than three-quarters of the eighty millions of the population of the Indian states. In addition, there are one hundred and twenty-seven states with an aggregate population of under ten millions, which are represented in the chamber of Princes by twelve members, elected by themselves. Beyond these are some three hundred and twenty-seven patches of independent territory, which are only classed as states because they are not part of British India.

The premier state is Hyderabad with a population of fourteen millions and a revenue of some five millions sterling. Next in order comes Mysore with a population of six millions and a revenue of two and a quarter millions sterling. The other Princes who have twenty-one guns, the highest salute given to an Indian Prince by His Majesty the King-Emperor, are Baroda, Gwalior and Kashmir which have a revenue each of about a million and a half sterling. In the eyes of the Hindus His Highness the Maharana of

Udaipur, the sun of all Hindus, the chief minister of God, ranks first because of his birth and traditions. No daughter of Udaipur was ever given in marriage to any of the Moghul emperors.

In the Indian states nature assumes its grandest and its simplest forms. The eternal snows of the Himalayas gather up and enshrine the mystery of the east and its ancient lore. The enterprise of old-world western adventure now slumbers by the placid lagoons of Travancore and Cochin. The parched plains of Rajputana and central India with their hilly fastnesses recall the romance and chivalry of days that still live and inspire great thoughts and deeds. The hills and plains of Hyderabad and Mysore, famed for gems and gold, for rivers, forest, waterfalls, still cry out great names of history. Over the dry trap plateaux of the Deccan swept the marauding hosts of the Mahrattas, eating here and drinking there, right up to ancient Delhi. From the west, the ports of Kathiawar with their busy progressive people stretch out hands to the jungles of Manipur in the east with their primitive folk and strange practices. The marching life of Moghul and Mahratta times has yielded to the sustained quiet of British rule, but the old spirit survives in many a story and many a hope.

The beauty of Kashmir has often been celebrated in prose and rhyme. One of the grandest sights in India is the fort at Jodhpur, built by titans, in Kipling's unrivalled phrase, and lit with the glory of the morning sun. It stands on a bluff over the town, like some great leviathan left high and dry by a subsiding flood. The holes in the masonry made by the enemy's artillery and the impressions of the hand-prints of the ladies of the ruling family, taken as they went to die on their husbands funeral pyre for the glory and honour of their house, recall the age-long pride and internecine struggles of Rajputana. The pink city of Bikanir rises out of a desert, part of which has now become fertile through canal irrigation. In Udaipur with its white marble palaces on the shore or on the islands of the lovely lake, reposing among russet hills, are treasured up and repeated stories of romance and sacrifice, of honour and of crime and curses, that revive the memories of an ancient world. The cave temples of Ellora with their gigantic figures carved from the solid rock, and the frescoes of Ajunta, draw visitors from distant countries to Hyderabad. The ruined city of Mandu with its Pathan architecture and walls twenty feet thick, stands on the edge of the central Indian plateau, and looks over the ghats to the Arabian sea. The sad deserted but lovely city of Amber in Jaipur, the Buddhist ruins at Sanchi in Bhopal, are both in Indian states.

Mysore contains the historic fort of Seringapatam on the east and on the west the Gershoppa waterfalls. These falls, at the end of the rainy season, are one of the most beautiful sights in India. In the background is a tiara of brown hills, in the foreground wooded slopes to the river, which races over boulders and rocks to roll over the cliff in four distinct streams. On the left, facing it, are the *raja* and the *roarer* tumbling down a hollowed shaft, a sheer drop of eight hundred and thirty feet; in the centre is the *rocket* bursting on a ledge near the summit into clusters of dropping foam; and on the right is a lovely cascade, *la dame blanche*, dancing down a buttress on the hill side, breaking into a thousand jets and eddies on ledges and knobs but re-forming all the while into a moving sash of spray.

The Indian states survived the establishment of the British dominion on the ruins of the Moghul empire and the Mahratta supremacy. By the end of the first quarter of the nineteenth century the British were supreme and unquestioned rulers of India. Writing of the political conditions of India in A.D. 1818, Sir Alfred Lyall said: "Henceforward it became the universal principle of public policy that every state in India (outside the Punjab and Scinde)" —these had not then been annexed—"should make over the control of its foreign relations to the British Government, should submit all external disputes to British arbitration, and should defer to British advice regarding internal management so far as might be necessary to cure disorders or scandalous misrule. A British resident was appointed to the courts of all the greater princes as the agency for the exercise of these high functions; while the subsidiary forces and the contingents furnished by the states placed the supreme military command everywhere under British direction."* Forty states have treaties made between them and the East India Company at different times; the others owe their position and security to engagement or recognition. Generally, the states have different degrees of internal sovereignty. The more important have powers of life and death over their subjects, of banishment from their states, of confiscation of property, of imprisonment for life. Their relations with external powers are in the hands of the British, who as paramount power control the succession to the rulership of the states, manage them for the princes during minorities, and have powers of intervention and, in extreme cases, of deposition of the ruler in the event of gross misrule, disloyalty, or crime. The British while protecting the rulers of the states have never divested themselves of their re-

* "British Dominion in India," Chapter XVI.

sponsibility for certain standards of administration in the interest of the ruler and the people of the states and of India as a whole. Intervention has been necessary from time to time. The Indian States Committee (1928) reported that in the last ten years the paramount power had taken action in eighteen cases, nine of which were classified as maladministration and five as gross extravagance or grave financial embarrassment.

There are many forms of constitution in the Indian states. The majority are under pure autocracy. The southern India states are the more progressive, but they, also, are ultimately under the absolute will of the ruler. Mysore was for fifty years under British rule and was then handed back to the ancient Hindu ruling family during the vice-royalty of Lord Ripon. The British methods of administration have been continued, a large measure of constitutional government has been granted and there is an efficient High Court of justice. Travancore and Cochin head the list in the education of the people and both are administered on modern lines, while Travancore has a constitution which seems to work well. Hyderabad and Baroda are under the absolute will of their rulers but are also governed on modern lines. The larger states can afford the salaries necessary to attract good men as administrators, but the position of those administrators is dependent on the will of the Prince. The consequence is an atmosphere of intrigue and rather general back-biting. An able and loyal public servant in an Indian state once observed: "There is no education equal to that of Indian state service. It cures one of ambition." Ordinarily there is a competition for the Prince's favour and a feverish anxiety to give him information before he gets it from another source. The subordinates are paid smaller salaries and the standards of administration are definitely lower than in British India. Even in the best governed states the administration of justice cannot compare with that of British India. On the other hand the system is looser than in British India, the taxes are recovered with less rigidity, there is a personal touch between the ruler and the ruled which is wanting in British India, and more is done for the amusement of the people, an important consideration which we have rather neglected. Efficiency secures the welfare of the many but is never very popular with the privileged few. "Never use that offensive word sympathy," a Bengalee friend once said to me, "it is a word of superiority. The only more offensive word in the English language is efficiency." The Indian states certainly do not as yet suffer from an excess of efficiency. Some twenty years ago the highest paid official in one of the smaller states drew a salary of less than ten pounds a month as inspector of prostitutes and was given an allowance of an extra pound a month for officiating as Chief Justice! That was an extreme case, no doubt, and there has been much progress since then. It can no longer be said, without much qualification, as Sir Madhav Rao once said, that while in British India the happiness of the people was the object of government, in Indian states the object of government was the happiness of the ruler and his friends and dependants. The tendency is to imitate the administrative system of British India, retired officials from which are frequently employed, but many of the institutions borrowed from this source are transformed in substance by autocracy. "What would happen," I asked the representative in London of an oriental kingdom, "if your democratic assembly refused to vote supply?" "They would probably be summoned to the palace," was his answer, "and after that they would vote it!"

As may well be imagined, the relations between the paramount power and the states are delicate and sometimes difficult. The paramount power is the Crown acting through the Secretary of State for India and the Governor-General in Council who are responsible to the British

Parliament. For every important state, and for groups of minor states, there is a local representative of the paramount power, called a resident, or political agent, a member of the political department. He is the mouthpiece of the British government and the interpreter to them of the wishes and sentiments of the Prince or Princes to whom he is accredited. On the whole political officers have done their work extremely well and earned the gratitude of the Princes. The impartial observer can hardly avoid the conclusion that but for the friendly help of political officers there would be far fewer Indian states than exist to-day. People are human. Not every Prince nor every political officer is perfect. The presence of a watch-dog in his state must often be disagreeable to a Prince but is absolutely necessary in the interests of the state subjects and imperial policy. The general character of the relations of the paramount power to the states has been well described by an eminent jurist. "The same people," wrote Professor Westlake, "has determined by its action the constitutions of the United Kingdom and of India, and as a consequence these are similar so far as that neither is an engine-turned structure, but the architecture of each includes history, theory, and modern fact, and the books which describe them are similarly varied in their composition. On the side of substance the principal difference between them is that, while in both the field covered by express definition leaves room for questions to arise, in the Indian constitution an acknowledged supreme will decides every question which arises, but in that of the United Kingdom a balance of power causes questions to be less easy of solution." The latest authoritative statement on the relationship of the states to the Crown is contained in Lord Reading's letter to His Exalted Highness the Nizam dated 27th March, 1926. This letter had the approval of His Majesty's Government. It has the imprimatur of Lord Birkenhead, ex-Lord Chancellor of England, as Secretary of State, and Lord Reading, ex-Lord Chief Justice of England, as Viceroy. The letter is a long one but the main conclusion is as follows:—"The sovereignty of the British Crown is supreme in India, and therefore no ruler of an Indian state can justifiably claim to negotiate with the British Government on an equal footing. Its supremacy is not based only upon treaties and engagements, but exists independently of them and, quite apart from its prerogative in matters relating to foreign powers and policies, it is the right and duty of the British Government, while scrupulously respecting all treaties and engagements with the Indian states, to preserve peace and good order throughout India."

The education of young princes is never easy and in India where they are surrounded by flattery from the time that they can understand speech it is exceptionally difficult. Many Princes owe much to excellent private tutors, English gentlemen, whom it would be invidious to mention, life-long friends of their princely pupils. Respect for his teacher is innate in the Indian's character. Chiefs' colleges have been established at Ajmere, Rajkot and Indore, with managing committees of ruling princes, which have done much valuable work. Many of the young princes have hereditary capacity. One of them when asked to write an essay on mountains produced something like the following: "Mountains are very good things, because where there are mountains there are forests, and where there are forests there are tigers, and where there are tigers Viceroys come to shoot, and then the roads are put in order and the Chief is made a G.C.S.I. and that is very good for the state." Another, when asked what he would do if he came to be a ruler and found his state heavily in debt, replied, "I should make great friends with the chief minister for a year and when I had got what information I could from him I should put him into prison until he disgorged." Those two observant young men had perhaps not much to learn from the conventional seminary. As a body the Princes have produced many fine characters and benevolent autocrats. Their loyalty to the Crown recalls the personal devotion of a younger age. Their splendid services to the British during the Mutiny, in the great war and on other occasions are matters of history. The majority are conservative but so are their people. More than fifty years ago Lord Lawrence was asked if people were happier in British India than in Indian states. *Bona si sua norint,* if they knew their blessings—yes, he replied, but he felt doubtful if they knew them. To-day one could hardly give a very different answer. There are some states in which a change to British rule would be welcomed by the people. In many cases the dislike of change would probably incline them to stay as they are. The Princes undoubtedly consider the welfare of their people much more than of old; and personal rule is attractive to most orientals. Let me have one master or be a master is their natural attitude. "Ten beggars can sleep under one blanket but two kings cannot dwell in one country" is an old proverb. But there is still need for many of the Princes to set their house in order, and particularly in regard to having a fixed privy purse for the personal expenditure of the prince, security of tenure in the public service for their officials and an independent judiciary. The desirability of these measures is accepted by the chamber of Princes in general, but the chamber cannot pass any resolution binding on its members, and there is at times, perhaps, a tendency to regard such resolutions as suitable for *other* states, unnecessary in one's own. Corporate feeling in the states is as yet undeveloped, but it may grow steadily and must be recognized and treated with imagination. Individual grievances will, it is hoped, be met promptly, and in a generous spirit, without waiting for constitutional developments, the maturing of which must take a long time. It may be added that the Princes are very tenacious of their privileges, very sensitive to any proposal involving interference in their internal sovereignty, very jealous of one another. Some of them are a little restive at what they call the undefined and unlimited claims of the paramount power over themselves; but on the whole the relations of the two, in spite of some difficulties of divided sovereignty, have, thanks to good sense and good feeling on both sides, been remarkably satisfactory and harmonious. Nowhere in the world to-day has autocracy so sheltered a position as in the Indian states under the suzerainty of the Crown. And this very shelter imposes on the British government an imperative and lasting obligation to protect the people in Indian states against serious misrule, for while in the days of insecurity the rulers of those states had perforce to conciliate their influential subjects in order to secure their following and support, this condition does not survive in anything like the same degree under the security of British rule.

IV

AN OUTLINE OF THE POLITICAL HISTORY OF INDIA FROM THE EARLIEST TIMES TO THE APPOINTMENT OF THE SIMON COMMISSION

THROUGHOUT her history India has been at the mercy of the invader. Over the north-west frontier, still vulnerable though heavily protected, Aryans, Persians, Greeks, Scythians, Huns, Tartars and Mongols have swept down on her rich plains, to settle or to destroy. All found the same conditions, a multitude of warring tribes, unable to combine, but intensely tenacious of their own traditions and culture. All sooner or later met the same fate in exhaustion of their virility by climate, or inter-marriage with the people of the country. All to some extent fell under the influence of the caste system, or the caste atmosphere. Even the British in their social life form something like a caste and have excited hostility on that account.

The Aryans had two periods of extended dominion, one before the other after the commencement of the Christian era. Not long after the death of Alexander, who in 326 B.C. overran the western Punjab, a great Aryan,

Chandragupta, established the Mauriyan empire (320—180 B.C.) in the north of India. He organised a standing army and a regular system of civil administration on, it is said, a Persian model. But even under his strong centralising rule Megasthenes, the Greek envoy to his court, counted one hundred and eighteen separate kingdoms. His famous grandson, Asoka (273 to 232 B.C.), who has been compared to our King Alfred, completed his work, embraced Buddhism, and carried it through southern India to Ceylon. His acts, edicts and precepts inscribed on rocks and pillars remain to this day. The next and last expansive Aryan government was that of the Gupta empire. This lasted from about A.D. 300 to 647, when it was overthrown by the Huns of central Asia. In the confusion which followed, the Rajputs founded small and isolated kingdoms. These periods, embellished by legend, are the golden ages of Hinduism. In the dissolution of the Moghul empire the Mahrattas attained supremacy, but as a loose confederation of states. The Hindu system with its caste divisions and priestly Brahman ascendancy did not, as M. Sénart has indicated, lend itself readily to the conditions of an extensive secular state.

The Moslems, on the other hand, were organised for expansion. By the beginning of the eighth century A.D. they had occupied Scinde. From about A.D. 1000 onwards commenced the series of invasions and conquests which culminated, after the battle of Panipat (A.D. 1526), in the establishment of the Moghul empire by Baber. Baber was the descendant of Tamerlane, who had himself sacked Delhi. A golden road from Samarkhand drew the Moghuls to India, and their empire filled the most brilliant period of her history before the British came; but there was almost constant fighting and the condition of the people at large was, by contemporary account, deplorable. The Moghul dynasty produced the human though cruel Baber, the great Akbar, wise and tolerant contemporary of Queen Elizabeth, the godlike builder Shahjehan, immortalised by the Taj Mahal—no mere building this, but a foam-like dream, a hope and a great desire,—and the forts at Agra and Delhi, and, lastly, Aurangzeeb, to Indians known as Alamgir, a learned, austere and strong ruler, who left behind him many wise sayings but who, by his religious bigotry and persecution, accelerated the fall of his house. To this day the minarets of the mosque which tower over holy Kashi (Benares), the site of a destroyed Hindu temple, remind the unforgetting and unforgiving Hindus of the fanaticism of Alamgir. His death in A.D. 1707 was followed by the steady dissolution of his empire. The Sikhs extended their victorious career in the north-west of India.

Powerful lieutenants of the Emperor, the Nizam of Hyderabad, the Nawab of Oudh, became independent. Hindu princes threw off their allegiance and Mahratta hordes swept over the Deccan, right up to ancient Delhi and beyond * and down to young Calcutta. The national hero of the Mahrattas, the great Sivaji, has quite recently been the recipient from Hindus of semi-divine honours. In A.D. 1736 Nadir Shah of Persia sacked Delhi and carried off the famous peacock throne. From this time onward, Afghanistan was severed from India. In A.D. 1761 the Afghan Ahmad Shah defeated the Mahrattas at Panipat, but was forced by his troops to return to Afghanistan. This was the last and fiercest of all pitched battles between Moslems and Hindus.

Meanwhile, a great maritime power had planted itself in trading settlements on the coast and was led on by events and the general confusion to establish its dominion all over India. The fabulous and real wealth of the Indies had attracted the Portuguese, Dutch, French and British in succession to Asiatic adventure. After conflicts between rival trading companies and maritime nations, the British prevailed by superior sea power and superior finance. The commanding genius of Clive and Warren Hastings

* "The Deccan horses had quenched their thirst in the waters of the Indus."—*History of the Mahrattas*. Grant Duff.

has received tardy recognition, but full justice has not yet been done to the statesmanship and capacity of the East India company. That company excited the jealousy of Governments and Parliament in England until, under Pitt, direct parliamentary control was instituted. It has been remarked that the Marquess of Wellesley was responsible for more high-handed acts than Clive or Warren Hastings, but escaped the criticism to which they were subjected, because he had friends at home. Unlike previous conquerors who came in from the north-west by land, the company had its bases in the south upon the sea. It moved its boundaries inland from the coast, feeling its way with alliances, spheres of influence and protectorates, absorbing territories under its own direct administration, or preserving local rulers under its political control, the successors of some of whom are the Indian Princes of to-day. It curbed impetuous and ambitious proconsuls, adapted itself to the requirements of Parliament and guided policy with rare practical ability and with due regard to finance, through all those difficulties which beset the foundation of a new dominion. Its methods described as "the rough and thoroughgoing methods of a stormy and dissolute period" were often questionable when judged by modern standards, but were quite conformable to the political standards of the place and time. It devoted steady attention to civil administration. It started public instruction, opened avenues of employment to Indians, encouraged their ancient learning and preserved their customs, although abolishing cruel rites such as human sacrifices, *infanticide, sati (the self-burning of the widow on her husband's funeral pyre)* and the organised crime of the bands of thugs who roamed over India strangling and poisoning their victims, with a fervour inspired by a sort of religion. It gave to India peace and prosperity such as she had never known. On the whole, the East India Company managed to avoid the rapid changes which act as extreme irritants to the east.* In its last days, however, it yielded to the pressure of impatient public opinion in England, preaching doctrines of a belligerent civilisation and practising domineering methods of reform. This was notably the case under the Governor-Generalship of a very great man—Lord Dalhousie—perhaps the greatest of a long line of illustrious men whom Scotland has sent to India. Over-confidence in western methods and ideals of government combined with disregard of military precautions were followed by the Indian Mutiny and the transfer in 1858 of the Government to the Crown, a reform inevitable, if not long overdue.

* "Hurry spoils curry," is an old colloquialism in India.

Opinions differ as to the causes of the Mutiny. According to Lord Lawrence it was a struggle between Christianity and civilisation on the one side and barbarism and heathenism on the other. "The wild fanatic outbreak of 1857," said Sir Alfred Lyall, "was reactionary in its causes and revolutionary in its effects. It shook for a moment the empire's foundations, but it cleared the way for reconstruction and improvement." To some it expressed the eternal conflict between Asia and Europe, the hatred of the Asiatic for the European and his desire, never long quiescent, to eradicate his influence. A wise contemporary—General McLeod Innes—attributed it in the main to the unrest caused by the annexation of Indian states by Lord Dalhousie, the overwhelming preponderance of the native army and the fear of the sepoys that their caste was in danger. Sir Syed Ahmad Khan, who lived through it, used to question the existence of any widespread conspiracy, or sentiment, and assigned the main cause to incompetent handling by inefficient authority. He compared it to a bazaar quarrel, which, if unchecked, spreads over the whole town. The forces of disorder are always near the surface in India and break out easily into violence and rapine. "India is quiet," Lord Lawrence once said, "yes, quiet as gunpowder." Asia is the land of revolution and revolution is in the blood of

India. Her history before we came is one long story of autocracy, tempered by corruption and corrected by revolution. Be the causes what they may, the Mutiny with its horrors and its heroism, its stern reprisals and its rich rewards to loyal Indian friends, was remembered vividly for two generations.

The moving language of Queen Victoria's proclamation and the feeling that once again they had a royal personal ruler profoundly affected the minds and imaginations of Indians. The capacity to take advantage of the charter of liberty and hope was, however, due to one of the last acts of the East India Company in the foundation in 1856 A.D. of the universities of Calcutta, Madras and Bombay. They trained up a body of Indian *public servants, lawyers and professional men* sufficiently imbued with western principles and knowledge to take a share in an administration conducted on western lines. Many Indian judges of the High Courts, the most popular institution in India, have attained the highest reputation. Then there arose gradually, but in increasing volume, a demand for the offices held by the British services which carried good emoluments and power. Progress in meeting this demand was slow, partly because the British services, recruited on covenant or agreement, had vested rights, partly because the number of Indians competent to fill their places was, in the early stages, few. The process of indianization was steadily developed and was finally reduced to definite system by the report of Lord Lee of Fareham's commission (1924).

The loaves and fishes of office were more sought after than self-governing institutions, but considerable progress was made in this direction also. Indians were associated in legislation and given powers of interrogation, statement of grievances, and voting supply. The chain began with the Councils Act of 1861 and was carried further during the viceroyalties of Lords Mayo, Ripon, Dufferin* and Lansdowne. Reform commenced with small committees to aid in the framing of laws and ended with legislative assemblies with

* The following story told me by Lord Macdonnell illustrates some of the difficulties of secrecy in India.

Mr. Macdonnell was secretary to Sir Charles Aitchison's Committee, appointed by Lord Dufferin to consider further political advance. While correcting the proofs of the very secret report, he was visited by an Indian gentleman. He became so interested in the conversation that he showed the visitor to the door of the house and returned to his room to find that the proofs had vanished. The premises were searched without result. When Mr. Hume, a retired member of the Indian civil service and the father of the Indian national congress, made a speech, showing evident familiarity with the secret report, Mr. Macdonnell wrote him a strong letter denouncing this use of tainted information. He received a reply to this effect: "Your letter has amused me very much. You forget that we theosophists have sources of information not yet recognised by western science." Mr. Hume and his sister were prominent theosophists in those days. In one of the Indian states about that time, the waste-

large powers of legislation, criticism of the executive, and voting supply. Electorates were gradually established. A new departure was the grant in 1906 of separate electorates to Moslems as a result of very powerful representation from that community which converted even Lord Morley against his will. The Minto-Morley reforms of 1909 were a definite step forward, and two Indian gentlemen were appointed to the Secretary of States Council and one to the Executive Council of the Governor-General. But the executive governments, central and provincial, remained responsible to Parliament, and were not removable by adverse vote in the legislatures. The government was still absolute in essence though influenced in increasing measure by the voices of the people governed. Both Lord Minto and Lord Morley expressed emphatic opinions that parliamentary government was quite inapplicable to Indian conditions.

Then followed an event of high political significance—the transfer of the capital from Calcutta to Delhi, announced to an astonished world by

paper basket of the British resident was regularly bought by the State from the residency servants for a monthly payment of five hundred rupees! One of my earliest tasks was to spend a day in the government press supervising the printing of examination papers. By many devices information is obtained of the questions set. One ingenious compositor had his white duck trousers heavily starched and sat on the type. From his bended person clues to some of the questions were obtained!

His Majesty the King-Emperor at the royal Delhi durbar on 12th December, 1911. Calcutta, the city of palaces, raised on a swamp by British, largely Scottish, enterprise, had long expressed in majestic outline the rise and expansion of the British dominion, from the first acquisition under Clive of the rich province of Bengal to the establishment of the British power all over India. In Calcutta were enshrined the proud memorials of a dominant race, and the living expression of British commerce and adventure. Calcutta produced a long line of great men, the latest and the greatest being the Earl of Inchcape of to-day. But the centre of political gravity had long shifted from Calcutta, geographically remote from the Indian states, the fighting races and the all-important north-western frontier. Moreover, the Bengalees, a people of lively genius, were in many ways isolated from the other peoples of India. Lord Lawrence and others felt it. Sir Alfred Lyall wrote in a private letter from Allahabad at the time of the controversies over the Ilbert bill: "The Secretary of State should at once order a residence to be built for the Viceroy in India outside Bengal—nothing can be worse for Viceroys than the present system of dividing time chiefly between Calcutta and Simla—at Calcutta the Viceroy is surrounded by eloquent baboos, at Simla by confident officials." The outbreak of the revolutionary movement in Bengal in 1907 brought matters to a head. Indian legislators from other provinces became infected by Bengalee ideas, and the local government was overshadowed and reduced to impotence by the presence in Calcutta, during the most important season of the year, of the Government of India whom the Secretary of State held responsible. I remember Lord Minto discussing the position with me and my suggestion that the Calcutta session of the Government of India should be divided, that a Viceroy's residence and council chamber should be built at Lucknow or Agra, and that all meetings of the legislature should be held there. Nothing was, however, done until Lord Hardinge took the matter up and pushed it through. Lord Hardinge's proposals gave expression at once to the growing feelings of India towards greater unity, and the need by decentralisation for a movement towards provincial autonomy. They included a revision of the partition of Bengal, an administrative act of Lord Curzon, popular with Moslems but deeply resented by Hindus. The secrecy and shock of the decision were necessary but occasioned bitter controversy except in Bombay and other cities long envious of the privileged position of Calcutta. The European community of Calcutta felt it as an outrage, the Moslems as the wound of an enemy, the Hindus rejoiced, but the Bengalees felt that they were paying a heavy price for their victory.* Lord Kitchener, long interested in the question, wrote to me from Egypt: "The change of government to Delhi will, I feel sure, consolidate our position in India and make its permanence felt by all the people. The idea of having the sea in close proximity for a possible retreat will vanish and Wellington's views on the subject are no longer necessary and need not alarm anyone." Calcutta is still a grand city and the proud accomplishment of New Delhi has stilled though it has not stifled controversy. The transfer of the capital marked the end of the old epoch and the beginning of the new. Henceforth the central government had a habitation of its own, free from any preponderant provincial influences. One result was not foreseen, the predominance of Bombay commercial influence over the Indian legislature and the central government, especially in the finance department, a tendency, perhaps, fostered by the absence of a clear united policy on the part of the European commercial element in Calcutta.

The great war followed. And then there came

* The editor of one of the leading Bengalee papers published in English said to me at the time: "You English are diabolically clever. You have ruined Calcutta and we have to thank you for it. Had we foreseen this we should have accepted the partition."

that freshet of happy-thoughtiness and gesture, conference and conversation, in apparent scorn of realities, which has ended in political and economic confusion. Indian loyalty touched the heart of the Empire. The Princes, indeed, responded magnificently, as did the fighting races of India, pre-eminently in the Punjab and also in a less degree in the United Provinces. Parliament, politically minded, decided to mark its gratitude by political concessions to the comparatively small educated class, whose loyalty had been less general and conspicuous.* On the 20th August, 1917, Mr. Montagu announced the policy of His Majesty's Government as "the gradual development of self-governing institutions with a view to the progressive realisation of responsible government in India." This policy was embodied in the Government of India Act of 1919 with certain conditions and safeguards. The progress was to be achieved by successive

* In 1915 an eminent Indian journalist asked my confidential opinion on Indian loyalty. If loyalty, I said, meant loyalty to the King-Emperor, all India might be said to be loyal. If it meant absence of a desire to get rid of the British, practically all India was loyal. But, I added, I think the educated class would like to see us humiliated without being beaten in the hope of political concessions. He laughed and added that his paper sold best when there had been a German success. Subsequent events have to some extent confirmed the accuracy of the diagnosis.

The Montagu-Chelmsford report noticed the deterioration of political feeling as evidenced by the proceedings of the Indian national congress in 1915 and 1916 respectively.

stages, the time and manner of each advance were to be determined only by Parliament, which would be guided by the co-operation received from and the confidence inspired by those on whom new opportunities had been conferred. From the first a hostile non-co-operating party was organised which steadily gained in power and as steadily increased its demands. In oriental countries safeguards and conditions are treated very lightly, and conditional promises to pay at a distant date usually set up claims for unconditional payment here and now.

Between 1917 and 1919 Mr. Montagu visited India and in conjunction with Lord Chelmsford produced a report, of which it was said at the time that the first or historical part contained a conclusive refutation of the proposals contained in the second part. Sharp controversy had arisen as to the meaning of the term "responsible government."* To the view that it did not mean parliamentary government was opposed the view that it could mean nothing else, and the latter view prevailed. The immediate result was the creation of dyarchy or double government† in

* From Lord Ronaldshay's "Life of Lord Curzon" it would appear that the term crept in without consideration by one of those inadvertencies of which political history is full. Lord Curzon, the author, or the borrower, of the phrase, disliked the whole system built up on it.

† The term dyarchy was first applied to the division of the Roman Provinces by Augustus between himself and the

the provinces. There are nine main provinces in India.* At the head of each province is a Governor with a cabinet, or as it is called in India, an executive government. The cabinet is divided into two parts. The one consists of Members of Council, officials or private Indian gentlemen, appointed for five years, responsible ultimately to Parliament, and in charge of the portfolios of "reserved" subjects—justice, police, prisons and revenue (the official subjects). The other consists of Ministers, selected by the Governor from members of the local legislature. The Ministers hold office at the pleasure of the local legislature and are in charge of the portfolios of the "transferred" subjects, education, public health, excise, agriculture, etc. (popular

Senate. In India it has almost become a term of abuse. I have heard one man shouting to another, "You are a dyarchy." "I will beat you with a dyarchy," said one Indian boy to another, and when questioned as to what a dyarchy was replied, "a new kind of tennis racket"! I have been received in a Burma village by a dyarchy band braying against a home-rule band with all the vigour of village faction, neither having the least idea what home rule or dyarchy meant.

*	Population in Millions.	No. of Members in the Legislative Council.
Assam	8	58
Bengal	49	140
Bihar and Orissa	37	103
Bombay	21	114
Burma	14	103
Central Provinces	15	73
Madras	46	132
Punjab	23	94
United Provinces	48	123

subjects).* The finance department is common to and in a sense above both sides of government. The Members of Council and Ministers are all heads of their respective departments and meet periodically under the presidency of the Governor, who has power to over-rule them in certain circumstances. The decision in the case of the reserved subjects rests with the Governor and the Members of Council, in the case of the transferred subjects with the Governor and his Ministers. Each side of the government is expected to advise and assist but not control the other. This executive government depends for legislation and supply on a legislative body with a large non-official majority, but the Governor has the power to restore supply refused by the legislature in the reserved or official subjects only.

The Government of India Act of 1919 was thus a large step towards responsible government. At the present moment the executive governments or cabinets of the nine major provinces contain eleven European and fourteen Indian Members of Council and twenty-three Indian Ministers. The provincial governments are thus already mainly Indian. This is a point often overlooked by hostile Indian critics! An Indian Governor was appointed but he could not stand the strain and resigned. Indians have officiated for a few

* The details vary somewhat in different provinces.

months since then. The craziest constitution will work if supported by experience and a sense of compromise: the wisest will not work without them. The general opinion has been that dyarchy failed because the legislature concentrated criticism on the reserved or official subjects, and shirked all unpleasant votes by leaving it to the Governor to exercise his special powers. It was also found that Ministers rarely resigned. This was hardly to be expected. The Indians in the beginning did not ask for responsibility. Before Mr. Montagu and Lord Chelmsford the joint scheme of the Indian national congress and the all-India Moslem league proposed an irremovable executive, the ancient and universal form of Asiatic government.

V

THE SIMON COMMISSION, THE ROUND TABLE CONFERENCE AND AFTER

THE preceding sketch of political history takes us down to the Montagu-Chelmsford reforms. These were embodied in the Government of India Act of 1919. It was one of the terms of that Act that at the expiration of ten years a statutory commission should be appointed "for the purpose of enquiring into the working of the system of government, the growth of education and the development of representative institutions in British India, and matters connected therewith, and the commission shall report as to whether and to what extent it is desirable to establish the principle of responsible government, or to extend, modify or restrict the degree of responsible government then existing therein." This Act is still the law of the land. And when it is remembered that the preamble to the Act laid down that "the time and manner of each advance can be determined only by Parliament upon whom *responsibility lies for the welfare and advancement of the Indian peoples,*" and, further, that in such matters Parliament must "be guided by the co-operation received from those on whom new opportunities of service will be conferred and by the extent to which it is found that confidence can be reposed in their sense of responsibility," it is very evident that the cries of broken pledges raised so loudly of late have no sort of foundation in reality. The pledges were strictly limited by conditions and those conditions have certainly not been fulfilled. On this point there is hardly room for controversy.

Before ten years had expired the parliamentary Simon commission was appointed, so called from its distinguished chairman—Sir John Simon. The commission was boycotted at once, not only by Mr. Gandhi and the congress, but also by most of the so-called moderates because it had no Indian member. Subsequently a commission composed of Indians was co-opted but its members were unable to agree on essential points and its many divergent reports have passed out of consideration. None the less the Simon commission made prolonged enquiries over two years in India. Before it reported, Lord Irwin declared with the authority of His Majesty's Government that, in their judgment, it is implicit in the declaration of 1917 embodied in the Government of India Act that the natural issue of India's constitutional progress as there contemplated is the attainment of dominion status. This pronouncement further complicated a difficult situation. In debates in both Houses of Parliament we were told that it meant nothing new, that dominion status was far away. In India, however, the effect was instant and dynamic. Dominion status was demanded at once. The Simon commission's report was condemned unread. The main proposals of that report were that full responsibility should be given in the provincial governments with powers reserved to the Governors to deal with emergencies, protect minorities and generally to maintain order and good government; but that the central government of India should remain irremovable and responsible to Parliament, not to any Indian legislature. The first volume of the report contains a brilliant description of India and analysis of the Indian political position. It has evoked the admiration of the civilised world and has already attained the importance of a classic.

The government then assembled a round table conference in London. It was not very round and it certainly was not representative. The most active political body in India, Mr. Gandhi and the non co-operators, refused to join it. The representation of the most important interests in India, the land, the fighting races, commerce, the army and the administrative machine was less than meagre. After several weeks of disagreement among themselves, they went away in good temper, thanks largely to the patience of the British parliamentary delegates and especially of the Prime Minister, the Lord Chancellor and Lord Reading. But they agreed to nothing except full responsible government in the provinces, as recommended by the Simon commission and a general approval of a federation between the Indian states and British India to which the Indian states committee and the Simon commission had referred as a possible though distant solution. But while the Simon commission insisted on the retention of parliamentary control through an irremovable central government of India, the round table conference after desperate disagreements recommended the introduction at the centre of just that dyarchy which had been condemned as a failure in the provinces. Defence, external affairs, the position of minorities, the financial credit of India and discharge of obligations and Indian states in regard to non-federal subjects were to be "reserved subjects" in the hands of the Viceroy, the other subjects were to be placed under ministers responsible to the Indian central legislature—no longer responsible to parliament. The rights of minorities and others were to be safeguarded, though no agreement was reached as to how this could be done. A new phrase was invented, responsibility with safeguards, and this was treated as a new political fact, although the safeguards were merely indicated and the responsibility was not defined. The Conservative party reserved judgment until a definite scheme had been produced, but the proceedings closed with many fragrant expressions of mutual regard. One result, indeed, was achieved. The round table conference undoubtedly gave the Indian delegates an impression of England's desire to help India such as they never had before. But its proceedings were shrouded in unreality. No definite scheme was worked out and everyone reserved his individual opinion. No attempt was made at any stage to visualise the effect of different proposals on the unrepresented masses of the people, and the minorities were left with a bitter feeling that they had been sacrificed to the Hindu majority.

Mr. Gandhi, who had been interned as a political prisoner for his open defiance of the law in his salt campaign, rather ridiculous to western, but far from ridiculous to eastern eyes, was released and called into consultation. Mr. Gandhi is no doubt a remarkable man. In 1921 he was a mahatma and appealed to the Hindu masses as a man whom government could not incarcerate because he had supernatural powers and would escape through the key-hole or in some supernatural way. When he was arrested in Lord

Reading's viceroyalty and could not escape from prison supernaturally, the masses lost faith in him. He was not a real mahatma. I was governor of the United Provinces at the time and the change in feeling towards him was apparent all over the province within three weeks. The government was stronger than Mr. Gandhi as he then became and has been since. He was no longer a Hindu with supernatural powers but a politician and, as such, did not attract the masses of the Hindus. It is hardly possible to convey to western minds the influence on Hindus of their ancient ideas. When the first aeroplane flew over Calcutta, I remarked to a Hindu servant on the wonder of it, and he replied at once, without any emotion, "In the days of Ramchandra the rishis (supernatural beings) used to fly." Mr. Gandhi may be a saint, but he is a very astute politician. His invention of the Gandhi cap was a stroke of political genius. It is a sort of skull cap of plain white material, far the cheapest head-dress ever known and as such appealing at once to the thrifty Hindu masses. Mr. Gandhi, as a politician, is much less formidable than mahatma Gandhi. As a politician Mr. Gandhi has scored a temporary success. The Gandhi conversations established him in the eyes of political India as the coming ruler of India. Of that there can be no doubt. Mr. Gandhi did what was natural in the circumstances. He assumed the position of a dictator.* Whatever else he may be, Mr. Gandhi is an adept in manœuvring position in the public view. He alone could represent the congress. He received deputations, rejected safeguards and criticised the government, which he had previously described as satanic. For a time there was a hope that the situation had improved but the impression was short-lived. A virulent attack on British trade continues. The round table conference was pushed aside, as the Simon report had been shovelled away, and new demands were put forward with recurring assurance. The Indian delegates who attended the round table conference were put entirely in the background. There is nothing surprising in this. Mr. Gandhi has long been in irreconcilable hostility to the British. For years now we have sacrificed prestige, position, interest in the vain effort to reconcile the irreconcilable. Governments have apparently ceased to govern as orientals expect them to govern. One of the delegates to the round table conference, an Indian of advanced views, said to me, "Some of your politicians say, 'Govern or get out.' But you can't get out and apparently you

* No Indian wants to be constitutional. "Every minister wants to be a maharaja," said one of the wisest and most detached Indians of his time, in reference to the Montagu-Chelmsford reforms.

can't or you won't govern."

True, the disorders though diffused have been confined mainly to the towns, and one or two localities near Mr. Gandhi's home. The Government of India reported on the 30th September last "a political agitation of remarkable intensity and fervour has left the rural districts but little affected." A statement that ten per cent. of the population of India knew that a round table conference has been in session might err on the side of exaggeration. Not ten per cent. of the population is literate in their own vernaculars. The intelligentzia who assembled for the round table conference are a very small minority. Only sixteen out of every thousand males in India are literate in English, only two out of every thousand females. They are an important minority and faith must be kept with them, but they do not as yet represent India. The masses themselves are deeply influenced by religion but care little for politics. Mr. Montagu and Lord Chelmsford deliberately set out to put this right, to disturb "the placid, pathetic contentment of the masses" as not being the soil out of which Indian nationhood would grow.* But so far their attempt has failed. The Government of India in their latest published report write: "The great mass of the people, though, as we have said, capable of being

* Para. 144 of their report.

galvanised into action by appeals on those matters which really interest them, regard with some indifference political changes which they do not understand."* There is no limit to the degree in which things can lend themselves in appearance to foregone conclusions of their character, but there is not even the semblance of anything democratic or popular in the federal executive to which Parliament is to surrender her responsibility for the welfare of the peoples of India. The federal executive will be, for very many years to come and until popular education spreads, an oligarchy of people out of touch with the masses to a degree not easily realisable by those who are used to western conditions.

It may be doubted whether the idea of federation can materialise quickly. Federation depends on the entry of the Princes and the agreement of the minorities. It will deal with federal subjects, *i.e.*, railways, aircraft, shipping and navigation, lighthouse, ports, posts, telegraphs, telephones and wireless, customs, salt, currency and coinage, public debt, savings banks, audit, commerce, trade, development of industries, opium, control of petroleum and explosives, geological and botanical survey, inventions and designs, copyright, emigration and immigration, central police

* Para. 11 Govt. of India's despatch on proposals for constitutional reform, 20th September, 1930.

organisation, control of arms and ammunition, central research, survey of India, meteorology, census, statistics, all-India services; immovable property in possession of the Governor-General in Council, the Public Services Commission. It was thought that the federal assemblies should be two—a comparatively popular assembly and a less popular senate. The Princes claimed for the states half the seats of the latter and something near half the seats of the former, although in population they represent two-fifths only. The Princes will allow no discussion of their internal affairs outside the federal subjects. On this point they are quite emphatic. "We know our states and our people," said H.H. the Maharaja of Bikanir; "we live amongst our own folk and are in the most intimate contact with their needs and possibilities. We shall know how and when to adjust our system to any changing conditions; but we shall do it in our own time and in our own way free from all external interference." The Princes apparently claim no right of discussion on purely British-Indian subjects outside the federal subjects, but wish to have a voice in the support or defeat of the federal executive. They claim further, it is understood, that federal laws shall not take effect in their territory until they have agreed to apply them, that their own subjects, even when guilty of an offence or wrong, under federal law, should be tried in their own and not a federal court, and that no federal officials should be employed in their states. Some of them seem to think that they will get a share of maritime customs and not pay much more to the federal government than they at present pay to the existing central government. Figures are not available, but undoubtedly the majority of states will have to contribute much more than at present they do, as the price of federal unity.

There is at present growing demand in British India that the subjects of the states should have representation in the federal assemblies. To this many of the Princes have strong objections. Some of them realise that they will be in a very exposed position if they enter a federation with British India in a permanent minority. They will find themselves in contact with some of the cleverest brains in British India, full of envy of the Princes and with interests not always, nor often, coincident with theirs. The Princes have not yet been able to federate themselves. They have, as a body, no experience of representative government. They are still for the most part protected autocrats, and they have hitherto relied on their protection. Moreover, there are some wise men in Indian states, who appreciate that, if the

Princes secure an independent tribunal as between themselves and the paramount power, they will not for long be able to resist a demand that there should be an independent tribunal as between themselves and their subjects. It is, in the circumstances, not surprising that many of the Princes should be cautious and shy of a radical change of status.

The Princes are, no doubt, able to look after themselves. What about the minorities, who amount in the aggregate to rather more than half of the total population of British India? They show no sign of agreement. It was, apparently, a surprise to some in England that the minorities were not able to settle their communal difficulties. The intensity of the Hindu-Moslem hatred is a commonplace to the Indian administrator. It is said sometimes that this bitterness is of recent growth. But serious riots between the Hindus and Moslems occurred in the United Provinces in the four years 1869-72, in 1886, and from 1891-95, long before political reforms came to the fore. And, of course, there have been many riots since. Enemies of the British say it is the fault of the government and cite the comparative rareness of the trouble in Indian states. The explanation of this contrast is simple enough. Autocracy prevails in Indian states and the ruler is either a

Hindu or a Moslem. He banishes at once from his state anyone who shows signs of stirring trouble. It may be added that quite recently there were serious riots in the constitutional state of Mysore.

There are many deep-seated causes of this antagonism. The Moslems and the Hindus have their own separate laws which profoundly affect their lives. They do not intermarry. The ordinary Hindu worships idols and to the Moslem idolatry is the grand abomination. The Moslem is a meat-eater and the only cheap meat is beef. To the Hindu the cow is immeasurably sacred and the slaughter of kine is the accursed thing. I have known a Hindu policeman weeping on duty because a cow was being slaughtered to his knowledge in the next street, out of sight. English education, honestly expected to unite the two communities, has proved in competition for appointments a cause of greater division. Again, the recent reforms with their opportunities for the exercise of power and patronage have further increased the hostility. Above all, the Moslems cannot forget that they were for centuries a ruling race and that the Hindus were their subjects.* Nor, in times of excitement,

* In 1911 (24th January) there was a fierce outbreak of feeling in the Imperial Legislative Council of Calcutta when Pandit Madan Mohan Malaviya challenged the special representation of Moslems. Those present on that occasion will

when the word goes round that the British will leave India, as has happened four times in the last forty years, can the Moslems put aside the hope that with the help of their co-religionists outside, they may re-establish their rule.

The tension between the two communities is a cause of much administrative inconvenience. Great precautions are taken to prevent their clashing, especially when their festivals coincide. Once feelings have been stirred the leaders lose all control over their people. Some unknown fanatic, a butcher, or a weaver, or a sweetmeat maker, takes charge. The actual outbreak may come in many ways, the slaughter of kine, though this is now regulated in most places by custom, the alteration of the route of a procession, the cutting of the branches of the peepul tree (*ficus religiosa*) sacred to Hindus, the use of music near a mosque, the blowing of conch shells by Hindus at inauspicious moments, the placing of a dead pig in a mosque by some bad character in the hope of disturbance and loot. The only

remember how in reply Nawab Abdul Majid of Allahabad hissed out the words: "It is only a century or a century and a half ago that Muhammadans were the rulers of this country: Hindus were the subject race of this country. How is it possible that people who have lost their sovereignty should be considered as having no political importance as compared with the people who were their subjects for centuries and centuries?" That feeling is even stronger to-day than it was twenty years ago.

safe course is to be absolutely impartial and stick rigidly to custom. As long as neither side scores over the other there will ordinarily be no trouble. A very wise district magistrate in the United Provinces kept the peace in his district for four years in succession by going into camp as soon as people became excited, saying that he could not settle any dispute that year but hoped to do so next year. His successor, scorning indecision, attempted a settlement which promptly led to a riot. Such instances could be multiplied. If either side scores an advantage, the women and the priests of the defeated side often take up the quarrel and force their men to active defence of their dishonoured faith. Boards of reconciliation are frequently appointed but rarely meet, or if they meet, adjourn *sine die.* Growing agnosticism may have some result, young men at college are often free from the extreme bitterness of communal feeling. But the competition seems insatiable. Lord Morley truly observed: "The difference between Mahommedanism and Hinduism is not a mere difference of articles of religious faith or dogma. It is a difference in life, in tradition, in history, in all the social things as well as articles of belief that constitute a community." And in any case the intelligentzia are very ill equipped to influence their co-religionists. The power lies elsewhere. Until one has learnt that every political question will be regarded through Hindu and Moslem spectacles from quite different points of view, one has not learnt the first essential lesson of India.

The recent horrors of Cawnpore, "the city of melancholy fame,"* with their unbridled savagery, will not soon be forgotten. It had its origin in the attempts of the Hindus to enforce a *hartal*, or closing of shops, on the Moslems and others, as a culmination of aggressive communal feeling. The last big riot in Cawnpore, about 1900, was over the unpopular government plague rules, designed to protect the people against the ravages of an unfamiliar pestilence. Then the rioters bound the policemen and threw them alive on to bonfires. The same savagery marked the rioting at Hardwar and Chauri-Chaura, the Moplah rebellion, the last big Calcutta riots which were communal in origin, and the recent riots in Rangoon which were racial between Burmans and Indians. The forces of disorder are very near the surface and easily break out in murder, rape, dismemberment, mutilation and other atrocities such as the cutting of the fœtus from the living body of a pregnant woman. These terrible outbreaks are often prepared. Bad characters, who abound in all the cities, are collected for the riot a day or two beforehand,

* "Cawnpore." G. O. Trevelyan.

and the fact of the riot is often known in distant places before the actual news of its occurrence is flashed along the telegraph wires. The significance of the recent outbreak can hardly be over-stated, coming as it does at the end of a period of exceptionally conciliatory policy and relaxed administration.

There seems to be equal reluctance on the part of the depressed classes, the Sikhs and other minorities, to welcome the new proposed constitution. The fact is that a strong Hindu revival is in progress. There have been many such revivals, religious or secular, in the past. A wise man of studied moderation, Sir Thomas Holderness, referred to the vague but deeply rooted sense of the Hindu of belonging to the soil and encompassing his conquerors. There is a passage in the speech made by Sir John Malcolm to the directors of the East India Company which might have been made many times, word for word, during the last century. The speech was delivered in 1824, when the stormy period of British conquest was over. Referring to the Hindus as "the unchanged people," he said: "They are to my knowledge adepts in spreading discontent and in exciting sedition and rebellion. My attention has been during the last twenty-five years particularly directed to this dangerous species of secret war against our authority which is always carrying on by numerous though unseen hands. The spirit is kept up by letters, by exaggerated reports, and by pretended prophecies. When the time appears favourable from the occurrence of misfortune to our arms, from rebellion in our provinces, or mutiny in our troops, circular letters and proclamations are dispersed over the country with a celerity that is incredible. Such documents are read with avidity. The contents are in most cases the same. The English are depicted as usurpers of low caste, and as tyrants, who have sought India with no view but of degrading the inhabitants, and robbing them of their wealth, while they seek to subvert their usages and religion. The native soldiery are always appealed to, and the advice to them is, in all instances I have met with the same—'Your European tyrants are few in number—murder them!' " Such notices were circulated freely at the time of the Mutiny. They were inculcated in the revolutionary movements of the Mahrattas on the west and the Bengalees on the east of India in the first decade of this century. These two revolutionary movements were at first independent of one another but preached the same doctrines, followed in both cases by assassinations. There have been other movements to encourage the idea that the British were leaving

India. The cow-protection movement of 1893 in the eastern districts of the United Provinces, which ended in extensive rioting, was conducted with great secrecy and took a form explosive against the government. British rule was in abeyance for some days. The Hindus appointed their own offices, imposed fines, established pounds for cattle and stopped altogether the reporting of crime. The marching of a British regiment through the affected area at once restored order and confidence. The tree-smearing movement was apparently inspired by the same purpose, to make the people think that the British were about to leave the country.* Mr. Gokhale, ordinarily very wise, when irritated, used to indicate that the goal of his people was to get complete control of the administration. Mr. Gandhi's civil disobedience movement was mainly supported by Hindus, and Hindus have led the attacks on British trade and commerce which are a feature of the recent discontents.

* This was a very singular movement never explained. The villagers in the early morning would find one or more groves in which every tree had a circle of mud with hair admixed. The government analyst reported that the specimens of hair sent to him were the bristles of a pig or the pubic hair of a fakeer. About this time I had a fakeer in my camp for about a fortnight. I learnt a lot from him round a camp fire and he was well cared for. One evening I referred to tree-smearing and that night he disappeared. In 1893 and on this occasion the tenants refused to pay their rents because a kshattrya raj was coming.

When there is a revival of Hinduism, cases of sati occur. There have been two such in Bihar in the last three years. On each occasion crowds of fanatical Hindus collected to overawe the police and witness the sublime and holy sacrifice.* There is undoubtedly a strong militant body among the Hindus opposed to all foreign influence and determined on reaction to the pure doctrine and practice of their ancient religion.

If inside India conditions do not look favourable for settlement, is there anything in experience in Asia to correct local apprehension? Western representative institutions have been tried and have not succeeded in Turkey, in Persia, in Egypt, in China. In each case there has been a reversion to some form of absolute rule. The case of Japan may be cited against this view, but the Japanese are a united and very patriotic people with old traditions of loyalty to government. "It was not an accident," said Meredith Townsend long ago, "that the Europeans have sought self-government and the Asiatics government by an absolute will." What has been the experience of our American cousins in the Philippines? The Philippines have a population of only twelve millions, mostly Roman Catholics with a Moslem minority, but none of the vast

* The report of one case will be found in the London *Times* of Tuesday, 5th February, 1929, in the proceedings of the Privy Council.

differences which caste and language and race make so prominent in India.

Under the high-stepping idealism of President Woodrow Wilson, the Filipinos were given almost complete autonomy. The results were so unsuccessful that General Leonard Wood and Mr. Cameron Forbes, eminent men with the highest local experience, were appointed to conduct an extensive enquiry in the islands. They found marked deterioration in the public service "due to the injection of politics," "a disquieting lack of confidence in the administration of justice, to an extent which constitutes a menace to the stability of government," dignified legislatures, but an absence of economic organisation and defensive power sufficient to maintain an independent government. They recommended that the Governor-General should have authority commensurate with the responsibilities of his position, that in the case of conflict between him and the Philippine Senate, the President of the United States should decide, and that in no case should the United States be left in the position of responsibility without authority. This was in 1921. General Wood was appointed Governor-General to clear up what was called the Augean stable. In 1923 some leaders of the Filipino government resigned and demanded complete independence, attacking

General Wood for undemocratic acts. In 1924 President Coolidge replied upholding General Wood and reviewing the situation at length. "The American government," the letter runs, "has information which justifies it in the confidence that a very large proportion, at any rate, and possibly a majority of the substantial citizenry of the Islands does not support the claim that there are grounds for serious grievance. A considerable section of the Filipino people is further of the opinion that at this time any change which would weaken the tie between the Filipinos and the American nation would be a misfortune to the Islands." The Filipinos owed much to the American government, their defence, their financial strength, their industrial and economic development. They could not stand the burdens of armament and governmental expenses, including a costly diplomatic service necessary for independence. Nor were they ready. "Working out the highest destiny of even the most talented and advanced of peoples is a matter of many generations." The responsibility for the Islands came unsought by the American people as the result of a strange and almost unparalleled turn of international affairs.

"In my judgment, the strongest argument that has been used in the United States in support of immediate independence of the

Philippines is not the argument that it would benefit the Filipinos but that it would advantage the United States. Feeling as I do, and as I am convinced the great majority of the Americans do regarding our obligations to the Filipino people, I have to say that I regard such arguments as unworthy. The American people will not evade or repudiate the responsibility that they have assumed in this matter." The very mission upon which they had addressed him was evidence that something was yet lacking in the development of political consciousness and capacity. So far from the executive exceeding its powers the legislature had trespassed upon the executive realm. "Looking at the whole situation fairly and impartially one could not but feel that if the Filipino people cannot co-operate in the support and encouragement of as good an administration as has been afforded under Governor-General Wood their failure will be rather a testimony of unpreparedness for the full obligations of citizenship than an evidence of patriotic eagerness to advance their country."

President Coolidge appealed to them to co-operate. He thought the conclusion inescapable that the Filipino people and not the United States had been the gainers from their connection during the last quarter of a century. The American government and people would gladly grant independence when the Filipinos would gain from it. "Frankly it is not felt that that time has come. It is felt that in the present state of world relationship the American government owes an obligation to continue a protecting arm to the people of these islands. It is felt also that, quite aside from this consideration, there remain to be achieved by the Filipino people many greater advances on the road of education, culture, economic and political capacity before they should undertake the full responsibility for their administration. The American government will assuredly co-operate in every way to encourage and inspire the full measure of progress which still seems a necessary preliminary to independence." And later on, for careful reasons given, President Coolidge disallowed a bill passed by the Philippine legislature to hold a plebiscite of the people of the Philippine Islands on the question of Philippine independence. And he laid down the following maxim of statesmanship—"The people should realise that political activity is not the end of life, but rather a means to attain those industrial and social conditions essential to a stable existence."* I have dwelt at some length with the experiment

* An exhaustive historical statement will be found in his book, "The Philippine Islands," by my friend Mr. W. Cameron Forbes. Houghton Mifflin Co. The Riverside Press, Cambridge, 1928.

in the Philippines because it exemplifies, or illustrates, although under conditions different from those obtaining in India, the complications and hazards of too rapid political advance in Asia.

VI

PARLIAMENT'S RESPONSIBILITY

THERE seems at present little prospect of agreement in India in regard to either the direction or the pace of political advance. The politically-minded portion of the population is so small, the non-politically-minded so vast. The lines of division are in the main religious and not secular, and religious antagonism continues to grow. Again, as already stated, the minorities together just outnumber the majority of caste Hindus but have little or no cohesion amongst themselves.* The educated few are crying for self-government. The masses of the people want good government. In our enthusiasm for goals we have almost forgotten to govern. We have lost sight of the claims on the administration to preserve peace and order and to administer justice promptly and without favour.

Those who have not been to India can hardly realise what administration means to the people

*	Millions.		Millions.
		Moslems	80
		Outcaste Hindus	75
Caste Hindus	170	Buddhists, Christians, Sikhs, Jains and Parsis	24
			179

at large. In this respect the whole outlook in India is quite different from that of western countries. In India government has to perform many services that are left to private enterprise in the west. In oriental phrase the sirkar, or government, is expected to be the ma bap, or mother and father, of the people. The administrative system dates from the days of Asoka, in the third century before Christ. It has been re-cast and reformed by the Moghuls and entirely re-fashioned by the British. The unit of administration is the district. There are two hundred and seventy-one districts in British India with a population averaging about a million each. The head of the district is the district officer, who is assisted by a district superintendent of police. These are the supreme embodiments of the government to the people. They are responsible for law and order and general prosperity. They tour about the district, find out what is going on, settle disputes, issue warnings, and give decisions that cover every aspect of rural life. They are the eyes and ears of the government.* Beneath them are three grades of subordinates, two of whom generally have magisterial powers, and each of whom

* The best description that I know of the position, activities and influence of the district officers is contained in pages 286—291, Vol. I, Simon commission's report.

controls and supervises the man beneath him. The lowest rungs in the ladder are the local subordinate police and revenue officials, the feet of clay as they have been called, who are ill paid and venal, and require much supervision.

Every year there are in British India about five million cases in revenue and civil courts of original jurisdiction, and some two million criminal offences come under investigation and trial. If for every case we assume that on an average five persons are interested as plaintiff, defendant, accused, advocate or witnesses, some thirty-five millions of people are every year directly interested in courts of original jurisdiction, in addition to the large number who come into contact with the local officials in purely administrative matters. Against this only some eight millions have the vote and less than half of them exercise it. These figures illustrate in rough perspective the relative importance of administration and politics to the masses of the people.

The small politically-minded class is divided like political parties elsewhere into two parts, extremist and moderate. The extremist demands complete independence, the withdrawal of the British from India, the extinction of their trade, and repudiation of all public debts. Its objects rest on race-hatred and its weapons are assassination and crime. All attempts to conciliate it have failed and have emboldened it to greater hatred and to fresh demands. This class originally modelled itself on the lines of Irish agitation. Ireland was the example and the ideal. In course of time Ireland ceased to satisfy. It was so easy to point out that Ireland was not like India historically or geographically. The fact of distance was one differentia. Again, Ireland is not divided into innumerable groups, unable to co-operate or understand each other's language, while India has not had in historical time any experience of self-government. India cannot be partitioned as Ireland was partitioned, because Hindus and Moslems and other antagonistic groups have perforce to live together all over the country. Above all, Ireland has not got a very vulnerable north-west frontier with all that this implies in external and internal policy. Be the cause what it may, the extremist now turns his face in prayer not to Ireland but to Moscow, the home and temple of hatred and revolution; and from Moscow he derives not only moral countenance but financial support. The moderate party, while afraid of the extremists, and careful not to offend them by denouncing their ultimate goal, prefers constitutional means of progress and wants naturally enough to hold office meanwhile. Both parties still base their ideas of progress on British models, but, of late, one or two thoughtful Indians have begun to question, or at least to wonder, whether it is possible to graft western democratic principles on the institutions of their ancient society firmly rooted in religion or caste. We shall not make the mistake that you have made, said a Hindu politician to a friend of mine, of letting the stupid people, referring to democracy, govern us.

Cawnpore reminds us that the first and most urgent need is to brace up the administration. There can be no doubt that the administrative machine has deteriorated of late. All accounts indicate that local officers are depressed and perplexed—if not in a state of apathetic despair. They are not confident of support. They see political considerations overriding even the administration of justice. Politicians have been allowed openly to break the law and go unscathed and this has a profoundly demoralising effect. The police in India cannot count on the assistance of the public as the police in England can. Under conditions of severe trial the police have done remarkably well on the whole, but they need constant encouragement and stimulus. They will need it more than ever now, because economic trouble is upsetting the countryside. Prices of agricultural produce have not been so low for half a century. When they sell or pawn their silver ornaments, in which their little capital is locked up, the peasantry get paid little owing to the present low price of silver. In the opinion of many competent persons this economic is more important than any political question and may at any time lead to agrarian trouble. The local governments are apparently looking to their revenue demands on the land to see if they are such that the people can pay them, and making arrangements to strengthen their police. Action also appears to be necessary in certain areas to stop the criminal intimidation by paid ruffians to prevent Indian dealers from selling British goods to Indians who want to buy them.

There should be no real difficulty in strengthening the administration. The government is immeasurably strong if only it will show its strength. It has at its disposal mechanical transport and good communications, air-craft and other developments of modern scientific armament. Sholapur, which had been in the hands of the rebels for a few days, was reduced to peace and order by a few hours of martial law, to the contentment, as it appears, of the great mass of the people of that town. The bulk of the people are law-abiding and expect government to maintain order. It is, of course, undesirable in ordinary times to rely too much on the military for the prevention of civil disturbance, but these are not ordinary times and the police force recruited in sufficient numbers for ordinary times may well require assistance in times of extraordinary stress. There is assuredly no reason for a feeling of defeatism in regard to India. Our prestige in some localities is no doubt at present rather worn and thread-bare, but it will revive, as on many previous occasions, when recent spasms of depression have passed away. Already, thoughtful Indians are criticising government for its want of firmness and demanding stronger action to prevent and suppress disorder.

As regards policy, Parliament alone can decide, and Parliament will be confronted by the difficulty of finding any party in India which can, in the language of the market, deliver the goods. Parliament has a high and honourable record. Through the Secretary of State Parliament has definitely and directly controlled Indian policy and Indian administration. British peace has brought countless blessings to India and a prosperity which she has never before enjoyed. It is probable that some two hundred millions have been added to the population in the last century; in the last decade there has been an increase of thirty-one millions. The development of the country has enabled India to support this huge population and have a considerable surplus of agricultural produce for export. When the Suez canal was opened in 1869 this surplus was eighty millions; in 1927 it was over two hundred and sixty millions sterling in value. A century ago there were hardly any communications. Governors-General travelled by river, or on elephants. Even in 1857 the guns had to be dragged up by hand to the relief of Lucknow; and the crossing of any large river was a formidable matter. Now there are forty-two thousand miles of open railway; some seventy thousand miles of metalled and more than twice this number of unmetalled roads; and most of the rivers have been securely bridged. Good communications are not only a great convenience to the people, they are a source of profit also. In spite of the pressure of population, there can be no doubt that the people are far better off than they were fifty years ago. The standard of living is low, but it is steadily rising. The consumption of wheat by the masses in the place of cheaper food grains has largely increased. Larger numbers travel by bus, car and train. More furniture is to be seen in the cottages and houses of the people; metal cups and vessels have largely supplanted earthenware; kerosene oil, mineral waters, cigarettes and black umbrellas are in common use. Considerable sums are placed in savings banks, and co-operative credit societies are steadily gaining ground. Famines used to be frequent and frightful when they came. The flesh of a son, said an old Moslem historian, of the famine of 1630, was preferred to his love. Now, famines are unknown. There is never a dearth of food, and periods of distress, due to bad harvests, are dealt with by codes providing work for the able-bodied and gratuitous relief for the infirm, which are a model of scientific administration. Great irrigation works have brought thirty million acres under irrigation and, since Lord Linlithgow's important commission, the improvement of agriculture is receiving increasing attention. The foundations of industrialism have been laid. The industrial census of 1921 showed fifteen thousand factories employing over two and a half millions of labourers. The bulk of the shares in the jute mills and in many other concerns run by Europeans is held by Indians. So far from England exploiting India for her own ends, as often alleged, India is allowed to impose a tariff against the import of British goods, a generosity now abused by a boycott movement. Some of the greatest engineering works of the world have been constructed by British engineers in India. Thanks to Lord Curzon and the archæological department, which he founded, the ancient monuments of India have been conserved and restored. Above all, the British have given hope where previously there was only fatalism. The poor have been protected against the rich; the tenants against their landlords; the depressed classes against those who for centuries have trodden them under foot. Education has been spread, hospitals have been erected and treat fifty million patients in a year; much has been done to improve public health.* There is still large scope for fresh endeavour in all these matters, but substantial progress has been made. The results in a backward agricultural country like India cannot be compared with similar results in advanced industrial countries of the west. And most of the progress in the west is only half a century old. A system of law has

* No country is satisfied with its educational system. There are limits to what education can take out that nature has put in, and to what education can put in that nature has left out. Education, like all social services, is subject to the law of demand and supply. In India, the people have not used their powers to tax themselves for education. Attempts to impose compulsory primary education have had a very partial success if they have not failed. In public health again progress must be slow. The plague rules were withdrawn under popular pressure. Health regulations affecting their lives and homes when carried out by subordinates are regarded by the masses in India as intolerably oppressive. "We do not wish to be sanitary," said the military colonists in the Punjab to Lord Kitchener many years ago. There has been steady progress since then, but great care is still necessary not to offend against popular susceptibilities. Nor should it be forgotten that the Hindus believe in a chain of existences. For them there is no death as we regard it. "To one that is born death is certain and to one that dies birth is certain."

been elaborated and the administration of justice has been purified. The independent High Courts of judicature, manned almost equally by British and Indian judges appointed by the Crown, are the most popular institution in India. All this has been done by British and Indians in co-operation, and the Indians have now been given an increasing share in control. The directing agency throughout has been Parliament acting through the Secretary of State, urging at one time progress, at another wise caution. The instruments of Parliament have been the splendid civil services of India relying on the great British and Indian army.*

Above all, Parliament has given India the first beginnings of an idea of unity, in spite of what one of the ablest of advanced Indian politicians has recently described as "the notoriously fissiparous tendencies of the Indian character." In the twelve main languages and the two hundred principal dialects of India, there is no word to express a unified India. Take away the British raj, said Lord Bryce, and the idea of unity will vanish like a morning mist. It is hard

* An admirable history of the Indian Civil Service has just been published—"The Indian Civil Service, 1601—1930," by S. O'Malley—John Murray. Having introduced the reforms in two provinces, I can say that without the loyal help of the civil services they would not have lasted many months.

to believe that Parliament will divest itself of its responsibility and its authority which must be commensurate with its responsibility. If a federal scheme becomes possible in the near future it may be hoped that the exercise of the safeguards, which will be necessary, will be left if not in the hands at least under the control of Parliament working through the Secretary of State. There will be many imperial matters the decision of which should not be left to a Viceroy in the heat of controversy and under the strong pressure of a federal assembly. If, as at present seems more probable, the idea of a federation is postponed and the only proposal left in the field is that of the Simon commission the question does not directly arise, for that commission maintained in full the responsibility of Parliament at the centre. This appears to be the vital question. All my experience in the government of India and in provincial governments convinces me that control of the provincial governments by the Government of India and the control of the Government of India by the Secretary of State are absolutely necessary for some considerable time to prevent India from splitting up into small units of low political capacity. In any case, as Sir John Simon has pointed out, the idea of federation which commended itself to the round table conference will run counter to experience of history. All federations of which we have knowledge, in America, in Canada, in Australia, in South Africa and in Germany, have been accomplished in the same way. The first stage has been the development of self-government in the separate states or provinces; the next stage has been the union of the separate states or provinces in a larger federal state by the sacrifice of some measure of local independence and authority. To reverse the process, to start a federation before the provinces have learned to govern themselves or the Indian states to have federated themselves, is surely to put the cart before the horse and is calculated to result in much confusion.

Owing to social isolation, which is partly of our own making, no doubt, but which is also largely due to the orthodox Hindu idea of the European as untouchable, and which is gradually being modified; and owing perhaps still more to the different economic standards of living, which are gradually being levelled, we cannot at present expect to be generally popular in India. But the people still prefer that their cases should be tried in the courts of British officers, and in times of trouble all classes turn to them and to the British soldiers for protection and help. And between individuals of both races great friendships are not uncommon. Two fixed points emerge through the heat and dust of controversy: (1) the British cannot go and, (2) India, without the help of the British, cannot at present administer or protect the country. Between those two fixed points some synthesis has to be found. We cannot go because of our obligations to India herself, the interests of the empire and the peace of the world, for assuredly if we withdrew the British army from India we should not only abandon India to chaos and internecine struggle but we should also create a vacuum which might well give rise to universal war. And apart from any question of self-protection, India cannot at present administer the country because of her divisions, the ignorance of the vast majority of her people and her inexperience of self-government. Her advanced politicians are asking in fact to attain in ten years a degree of political progress which it took us centuries to evolve, and our dominions, with our experience behind them, at least a century to claim. If anyone captivated by eloquence and superficial developments inclines to the belief that in India all things are becoming new, let him drift in a barge down the river front in the early morning at Benares, with its palaces and temples, its shrines and its burning ghats, its priests and ascetics, its mysterious practices and multiform ritual, its animal life, the monkeys, the goats, the sacred bulls, the whole apparatus, as it has been called, of higher and lower Hinduism, unchanged through the centuries, untouched by the west. Let him study the evidence and the report of the Indian age of consent committee. Let him reflect also on the recent horrors of Cawnpore and other outbreaks of pure savagery. Then it may be he will realise more clearly than before the immensity, the diversity, and the insistence of India, the difficulties of accelerating constitutional growth on western lines, and the need for many years to come of guidance and control by the British Parliament.